YOU'LL NEVER BE YOUNGER

YOU'LL NEVER BE YOUNGER

*A Good News Spirituality
for Those over Sixty*

WILLIAM J. O'MALLEY, S.J.

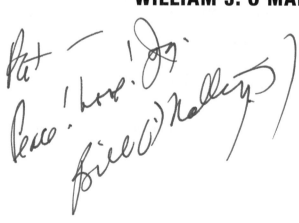

ORBIS BOOKS
Maryknoll, New York 10545

Founded in 1970, Orbis Books endeavors to publish works that enlighten the mind, nourish the spirit, and challenge the conscience. The publishing arm of the Maryknoll Fathers and Brothers, Orbis seeks to explore the global dimensions of the Christian faith and mission, to invite dialogue with diverse cultures and religious traditions, and to serve the cause of reconciliation and peace. The books published reflect the views of their authors and do not represent the official position of the Maryknoll Society. To learn more about Maryknoll and Orbis Books, please visit our website at www.maryknollsociety.org.

Manufactured in the United States of America
Designed by Roberta Savage

Library of Congress Cataloging-in-Publication Data

O'Malley, William J.
  You'll never be younger : a good news spirituality for those over 60 / William J. O'Malley, S.J.
    pages cm
  ISBN 978-1-62698-124-9 (pbk.)
    1. Older Christians—Religious life. 2. Christian life—Catholic authors. I. Title.
  BX2372.O43 2015
  248.8'5—dc23
                                                    2014029322

I don't call you servants any longer. You are my friends.
—John 15:15

For
David Murphy

Contents

Introduction: 11:37 p.m. at the Ball   1

1. Dignity   7
2. Attitude   20
3. My Soul = Who I Am   23
4. Staying Hungry   27
5. Perspective   30
6. The Fifth Dimension   35
7. The Joy of Imperfection   43
8. Genuine Humility   47
9. Incarnational Reality   52
10. Humor: Accepting the Absurd   58
11. Praying as an Adult   70
12. Gratitude   75
13. Empathy   79
14. Kindness   85
15. Loving   92
16. Curiosity   99
17. Enchantment   105
18. Choosing the Inescapable   111
19. Faith Means Confidence   120
20. Tolerance for Ambiguity   131
21. Beyond Authorities   141

22. Spendthrift Forgiveness 152
23. Eternal Life—Now 165
24. And Then? 174
25. Resilience 181
26. Letting Go without Quitting 192

Introduction: 11:37 p.m. at the Ball

*We've borne the burden of the day and the
scorching heat.*

—Matthew 20:12

Chesterton imagines Cinderella approaching her Fairy Godmother as the hour hand creeps to the crucial twelve and asking, a tad petulantly, "Why must I leave the ball at midnight?" He
suggests her lovely benefactress might reply with something like,
"Sweetie, who said you could *come* to the ball in the first place?"
Good for her.

If Cindy used the good sense God gifted her with at the start,
she just might have the wits to grasp the truth: if her time's dwin-
dling, she ought to get back in there and dance her crystal boo-
ties off while she still has some time. These are *the* most precious
minutes she has!

Even truer for those of us approaching "my three-score years
and ten" (which, if you need footnotes, is seventy). Even more true
for those of us who have exceeded the eighty-one years for women
and seventy-six for men assumed by life insurance companies. Every human being is, truly, "on borrowed time." But those of us in
the market for Botox are long overdue. Since we did nothing to
deserve all that extra time, it's idiotic to feel apprehensive about
it—much less guilty. But—just like the chance to be alive in the
first place—the privilege of getting old is an inestimable *gift*!

No matter how old I've gotten—if you want to reckon eighty-
two as "old"—I continue to be amazed at how many people
spend their entire lives in complete ignorance of how lucky
they've been all along. Just to be at the ball! No matter how
briefly. Even if you got a table by the door to the kitchen. Even
if somebody else was—from the get-go—wealthier, smarter,
handsomer, more charming, gifted, luckier. Wow! Even if your
only excuse for being here has been to bus tables or check the
prom queen's fur or wipe up the dazzling quarterback's spilled

vichyssoise. You can still enjoy the music—as long as your bruised ego doesn't block it out. And, whatever, it beats the hell out of being out there shivering in the parking lot. Not to mention never having lived at all.

The core premise of this book is the belief that "people around my age," people who underwent Christian training from the 1930s through the 1960s, were indoctrinated to the radical belief that, if you suddenly realize you've got only twenty-three minutes left at the ball, you'd best get down on your wobbly knees and make a damn thorough general confession of your whole life, scrupulously certain you left out not a single fault—no matter how shaming or trivial. Even the ones you thought had been forgiven. We were trained to worship—and fear—not the loving father who welcomes the prodigal or the Jesus who guarantees forgiveness 490 times (70 × 7), but a Dickensian moneylender who holds the keys to the debtors' workhouse and will release no one until the last farthing is paid—either in unspeakable suffering or tireless pleadings.

If you don't feel the slightest twinge of atavistic fear hearing that in your deepest memory of childhood and youth, ask for a refund for this book and read pros like Catherine of Siena, who quotes God telling her, "Your capacity to sin can never exhaust my capacity for mercy." Or Jesus who *never* said, "Ya better watch out, ya better not cry," but instead, "The thief comes only to steal and kill and destroy. I came that they may have life, and have it abundantly" (John 10:10).

In the final act of Thornton Wilder's *Our Town*, Emily's allowed to go back from death for a single day, her twelfth birthday. She's stunned. Everybody is so . . . "accustomed." So frozen in lifelong habits. So fortified against the magic of being alive. She asks the Stage Manager, "Do any human beings ever realize life while they live it? Every, every minute?" And he answers, "No . . . The saints and poets maybe—they do some."

What *makes* them saints and poets is realizing how gifted they've been. Part of the reason for this book is to stir up gratitude in those who've taken the gift of life for granted. Or who rebel against it as a burden. Any sane person over fifty who wakes up *any* morning should say, "Wow! Thanks again!" Even if it's raining. Even if their joints ache. It beats a coma!

At A.A. meetings, people often say what a lousy day they've had or what a "bad place" they're in at the moment. When it's my turn, I usually say that my continued sobriety—and thus my continued sense of fulfillment—comes from never, ever, ever asking myself what kind of day I'm having or what kind of mood I'm in at the moment. Never! I'm *alive*, dammit! As Carlotta belts out in Sondheim's *Follies*, "I'm still *here!*" And that's the very best gift of all.

This is the best there is—at least (if the gospel is dependable) until we get "There," which is reputedly even better than here. There—although no one's come back with specifics—nothing wears out, people don't find others they love better or lose interest or move away. No more deadlines, deadbeats, dead ends. In fact, no more dead anything.

When anybody asks, "How ya doin'?" I answer, "Better than I deserve."

If it's the first time I've pulled that on them, they say, "Well, of course you deserve. . . ." What? After the sine qua non gift of being here at all, what can I claim to deserve? That I refused to kill myself, like Sisyphus? (Google that name. He's a fine model—if you have no other motive left.)

Before birth, I didn't exist. How could a nonexistent deserve anything? It was entirely, utterly a gift undeserved. (Which is what "grace" means.) To start way (way!) back, God had no need to concoct and explode this multiwondrous universe. But he did. Nor would he have been less perfect without vegetation or animals. Surely, he should have stopped longer and reconsidered before he gave in and created humans—the absolutely only species that can refuse to do his bidding, the only ingrates who can tell him to get lost. But he did. And God was under no real pressure to give *me* a chance. But he did. Impossible to count how many people much worthier than I didn't wake up this morning. But I did.

In a word, "Wow!" That's a really great prayer: "Wow!" It praises the Tireless Giver.

Granted that, had I never existed, I'd never have been the wiser.

But I do exist—which surely *ought* to make me the wiser. At least wiser than a witless rock, or rutabaga, or orangutan. And it should leave me stunned with gratitude. When I feel the seductive pull of self-pity (don't dare tell me you don't), I really ought to sit down with a piece of legal-sized paper and list all the people I've loved— and been loved by—all these years. No matter how briefly they were "mine." How lucky to have known them at all! When that joy thins down, I ought to start another page and list all the *things* that have given me joy: babies, books, beer, bakeries, bubbles, brass bands, breakers . . . breathing! And that doesn't make a ding even in the "B's"!

In a word, "Wow!"

Along the way, I confess that I've misused many of those gifts, denied the dignity hardwired right there inside them, and tried to change their uses to my own ill-considered desires. Not just an ingrate about *having* them but about *using* them properly. Sometimes, I've been given the extra grace of insight to recognize my folly and the even further gift to ask forgiveness. But then, on top of everything else, the gift of still being *accepted*, no matter what. As the hymn exults, "And when I think of God, his Son not sparing, sent him to die, I scarce can take it in!"

Oh, yeah. And besides all that! That glorious Son endured ungodly torment and degrading death—not to buy back the love of God but to prove there's nothing at all we can ever do that could extinguish or even short-circuit that implacable love. God loves us helplessly—it's his nature—like a mother loves her child, even on death row. Catherine of Siena saw it. God assures us that our capacity to sin can never exhaust his capacity for mercy.

And it doesn't even stop *there*. He also came back from death. To show conclusively how inexhaustible his loving is, our Benefactor feels compelled to keep loving us—and to keep us loving back. All over the place. Even after death.

How could anyone as gifted as I've been get peckish when I ask for even more and don't get it? Any parent of such a child would feel there's quite a bit more teaching left to do. That's the only reason for purgatory. Not that there's still unworthiness to punish away. Purgatory is to refurbish souls who were too cramped, who failed to ready themselves for joy. Which is what heaven is all about. In heaven, joyless people would be like Bedouins at an ice-skating rink.

Forget Dante—who had no more right than I do to specify purgatory as dramatic punishments—since neither of us visited there. Our pictures of a way station to heavenly bliss quite likely depend on what kind of Father we believe God is. Despite Dante's evident genius, I'd picture purgatory as a place of "soul realignment," rather than corporal punishments. Many will find the experience of being humbled, "put in their place," as painful to the ego as the arrogant carrying heavy burdens to bend their heads or the envious having their eyes sewn shut with barbed wire *à la* Dante. I now suspect God is more elegant than a conniving Machiavellian overlord.

The scrupulous have to learn to laugh at themselves, maybe starting with just being tickled. Or pickled. World beaters need to teach patty-cake to infants who died in childbirth. Perfectionists are set to fish or paint still lifes. The judgmental may be taught to juggle Dresden china. Puritans will be taught utterly useless skills like dancing and jumping for joy.

The final years of one's life are to obviate that need to be slowed down by purgatory from getting to everlasting joy—simply by learning right *here* how to be capable of joy, serenity, not being God. Being comfortable with God before we leave this circumscribed ball for the real one. Because the Host, here and there, isn't the nitpicking God I learned to fear at St. John the Baptist School, but the father of the prodigal Son Jesus revealed.

If you actually believe all that stuff, then it really ought to show, shouldn't it? Those less aware of their own giftedness should suspect—just by looking at the way you live—that you know something they don't, no?

Charisms Count

The Pontifical Council for the Laity of the Catholic Church wrote something for people of all religions and none in *The Dig-*

nity of Older People and Their Mission in the Church and in the World (October 1, 1998):

> Old age grows with us. And the quality of our old age will especially depend on our capacity to grasp its meaning and appreciate its value both at the purely human level and at the level of faith. We therefore need to situate old age in the context of a precise providential scheme of God who is love.
>
> The contribution that older people, by their experience, can make to the process of making our society and culture more human is particularly valuable. It needs to be encouraged by fostering what might be termed the charisms proper to old age.

Easily said. But just what *are* "the charisms proper to old age"? Where do I find them?

Come and see.

1.

Dignity

Then God said, "Let us make humans in our image, after our likeness. And let them have dominion over the fish of the sea and over the birds of the heavens and over the livestock and over all the earth and over every creeping thing that creeps on the earth." So God created humans in his own image, in the image of God he created them; male and female he created them.

—Genesis 1:26–27

Each of us has a dignity bestowed—*not* merited or earned—by the fact God created humans with more going for us than the skills and faculties he gave other animals. If God failed to give us the ability to fly like simple sparrows or run fast as cheetahs or swim endlessly underwater like dolphins, he gave us the wits to make machines to do that for us. No animal we know can write "To be or not to be" or "E = mc²." If another ice age comes, we needn't drag ourselves as far as we can then just die, like other animals; we use elevated cunning to make fire, take pelts from other animals, and survive. Other animals know facts; we have at least the potential to *understand*. No other species is free to "do wrong," no other is burdened with conscience. We're a quantum leap more precious and worthy (just from the way we're made) than the nearest contender.

The Declaration of Independence acknowledged (it did *not* bestow) that unarguable difference: "We hold these truths to be self-evident, that all men are created equal, that they are endowed by their Creator with certain unalienable Rights, that among these are Life, Liberty and the pursuit of Happiness." Not because we're Americans. Because we're humans. Those noble rights can never be legitimately taken away nor surrendered. *Nor earned.*

What's more, no wolf can ever be more vulpine, no pig less porcine, no lion more leonine. But every newspaper reminds us of the vast spectrum of "humanity," those just over the line from beasts—pimps, pushers, hit men—through the rest of us, to incandescent examples like Thomas More, Abraham Lincoln, Sojourner Truth, Dorothy Day, Nelson Mandela.

Just as we alone of all species can degrade ourselves—act like beasts, vegetate, use others as stepping stones, we alone can overcome challenges and rise to a self-possession and stateliness that belie whatever our evolutionary origins were. We can become more than animals. We can even evolve ourselves beyond merely *rational* animals. We are souls. We can even outgrow our faulty socialization. *Even* our less than perfect religious learning.

Genuine Pride: Unshakable Self-Esteem

The only kind of dignity which is genuine is that which is not diminished by the indifference of others.

—Dag Hammarskjöld

Before there was Malcolm X, before Medgar Evars and A. Philip Randolph and Rosa Parks, even before Dr. Martin Luther King Jr., there was Jackie Robinson. He gritted his strong white teeth long before any of the other modern greats, and he took a heroic swing against indignity. Born in 1919 to Georgia sharecroppers, he and his four siblings were supported by their single mother, who cleaned other people's houses. "I had a lot of pride in her," he said later. "She'd work so hard, and never complained, to make us all feel happy."

He won three athletic letters in technical high school and then was an All-American halfback at UCLA. During World War II, after basic training, he applied for Officers' Training School, but even though he had almost completed college, he was rejected at first. He was black. From the army, Jackie went to play with the Kansas City Monarchs baseball team in one of the Negro Leagues. It seems ludicrous that a country that had just made untold sacrifices fighting a war to confront inhuman racial policies in Europe could still have "Colored Only" rest rooms, waiting rooms, even drinking fountains back home. But for a great many—even African Americans—that was simply the way things were.

An Obi-Wan Kenobi appeared in his life, a white man named Branch Rickey, president of the Brooklyn Dodgers, who vowed to wear down the racial wall in sports. The player he was looking for had to have more than athletic ability. He would need the inner courage and unshakable self-esteem to withstand all kinds of degrading abuse. The man he chose was twenty-six-year-old Jack Robinson. When Rickey met him, Jackie asked, "Mr. Rickey, do you want a ballplayer who's not afraid to fight back?" and Rickey answered, "I want a player with guts enough not to fight back."

In his first game, April 1946, as second baseman for the Montreal Royals in Jersey City, he scored four runs, drove in three, stole second, then third, then home. But it was otherwise uphill. In many cities, he had to room and eat alone in separate hotels and restaurants. Some ballparks refused to let him play. In Syracuse, a player threw a black cat on the field and yelled, "Here's your cousin!" In a game against Philadelphia, a chorus of venomous racial abuse poured out of the Phillies dugout, led by their manager. Jackie just kept taking deep breaths and clenching his jaw. Of the Little World Series in Louisville, he later wrote, "I had been booed pretty soundly before, but nothing like this. A torrent of mass hatred burst from the stands with virtually every move I made." One commentator wrote, "He was the only gentleman on the field."

But his teammates came round. So did the Montreal fans, who poured out to support a man they'd taken to their hearts, despite their reluctance. At the end of the final game, they carried Jackie around the field on their shoulders, "probably the only day in history," a sportswriter wrote, "that a black man ran from a white mob with love instead of lynching on its mind."

In 1947, when Rickey finally brought Jackie up to the Dodgers, bigots sent letters threatening Jackie's life. The team members suggested they all wear his number so no one could tell which one was black. The *Sporting News* named him Rookie of the Year. In 1962, after he had retired, he became the first black ballplayer to enter the Baseball Hall of Fame.

Jackie Robinson often told young audiences, "A life isn't important except in the impact it has on others." And throughout his life he believed "the most luxurious possession, the richest treasure anybody has, is his dignity."

Your life has, surely, done that. But can we retire from that human—humanizing—task?

You've probably never suffered the indignities endured by the truly great human souls—Abraham, Moses, Jesus, Socrates, Galileo, Gandhi. But if you've lasted around a half-century, over and above the respect you deserve as an image of God, you deserve respect simply for not having quit! You and I have *earned* a further measure of dignity. After all, we got through *adolescence*, didn't we? Beyond infatuations? Wrestled honest love out of romance? Learned to be content with far less than perfection, yet still eager for more?

You no longer have to prove yourself or market yourself. You're no longer a confused kid, a bewildered newlywed, a worried provider. You're the best self you *could* have made (so far), given what you had to start with, given the shape you were in when you met each of the ogres and dragons you've encountered along the way. You fell but you didn't fall apart! You did try your best. What reasonable God (or self) could ask more? Reluctant as you might be to admit it, God is saying to you—"Blessed are you among women" and "You are my son in whom I am well pleased." The proof of that is you're still reading this book!

You have a right to possess—to *be*—a serene soul, a self you've learned to trust—and have every right to trust, because—without even realizing, you've *proven* it—exactly the way Dorothy in *The Wizard of Oz* proved the magic in the ruby slippers all along was Dorothy herself.

Not everything in you fits perfectly, like a sphere, which is boring. Some rough edges still, lopsided bumps and scar tissue, but it all holds together. Being adult has finally gotten to be more comfortable, like mastering walking or riding a bike or learning to cherish a colicky child.

I dare you to test that out. Next time you encounter a snippy clerk, ask, "Do you take a nastiness test to get your job?" Or more effectively, "Where's the manager?" You know by this time in life, the clerk *deserves* it. But you deserve it, too. And it'll tickle your soul! Justifiably!

At the first-act finale of the musical *La Cage aux Folles*, Albine, an aging transvestite, is about to reprise "We Are What We Are," a kootch number the chorus has earlier danced. But just as he's going onstage, he's told that the boy he's raised, cared for, and coddled for twenty years (far better than his absent mother could have) has refused to allow him to meet his fiancée and her parents. The boy's ashamed of his "mother." With an imperious wave, Albine holds back the chorus and strides onto the stage alone. Jaw set, he begins the song, slowly, ferally: "I . . . *am* . . .what . . . I . . . *am*. I am my own *special* creation. . . . I am what I am, and what I am needs no excuses. . . . Life's not worth a *damn* till you can shout out loud I *am* what I *am!*"

Albine isn't gay in the sense of carefree. On the contrary, at the moment he feels belittled and betrayed, but he's unbowed. He's fought his way through a hell he didn't choose and made the most of what he has, at least according to his lights. His is an anthem of unapologetic self-acceptance and self-assertion, which not many can even comprehend, much less take to heart.

That's what this book hopes to bring to those who deserve such pride but are reluctant to accept the gift they are worthy of. The reason for reluctance for many Catholics is well meant but crippling religious training that completely garbled the true meanings of pride and humility.

The Greek word *hubris* in scripture is cruelly mistranslated as "pride," but to the ancients, *hubris* did *not* mean the justified self-esteem of Jackie Robinson and Albine. On the contrary, it's the narcissism and self-absorption of Oedipus, Nero, Hitler—arrogance almost no Catholic of our generation could ever achieve. We have too many inbred controls. We've heard too many times to count, "Now, don't you be *vain!*" As a result, many came away from childhood with the same enfeebling simplification of "pride," to the point of self-detestation. Cradle Catholics of our generation kept psychiatrists in business. (What will they do now that entitlement has exiled guilt?)

Conversely, with "humility," we were force-fed stories of saints who exulted in humiliation—to a point seldom short of masochism. Immediately after his adult conversion, Ignatius Loyola monomaniacally punished his vanity to a hideous degree, refusing to bathe, or cut his nails or hair. Until he was jerked to his senses and realized he wasn't being a saint but a posturing fool.

The root of the word "humble" (and of "human") is *humus*, "dirt." And it doesn't mean "filth" or "pond scum" but the good earth out of which Yahweh formed Adam and breathed a soul into him. The more fitting translation of both "humble" and "human" is "down-to-earth," feet-on-the-ground, clear-eyed, confident. It's why I picture Jesus as a big-boned Australian guy, not the pale wimp in the holy pictures with the doe eyes of an innocent novice nun. That's not "humble." That's "naive, clueless, out-of-it." Nowadays, kids are smart enough to see that.

It's of crucial importance to see the stark difference between genuine *self-esteem*, on the one hand, which is based on objective evidence—a consistent attempt to strive for one's best and to ride herd on petty meanness—and, on the other hand, *self-absorption* (narcissism), which is based on subjective illusion—a series of disguises, lies we tell ourselves, about ourselves, and believe!

Self-esteem depends on approval from *within*, conviction that, despite minor failings here and there, I'm honestly trying to do my best at everything I attempt. Its rock foundation is *honesty* about oneself. Self-absorption depends on approval from *without*, from convincing others (and myself) that "I'm OK!" even when I'm in fact *not* OK, when I consistently slack off, do the minimum, lie and cheat when I'm in a pinch. "I'm an honest person. I cheat *only* when I have need and opportunity!" Its foundation is nonexistent, since it consists in a continual series of flights from the objective truth—which is the only place in which to ground any belief.

That hollow, false self—(*persona*, mask)—is why many want diplomas, rather than learning, read self-help books, sign up for Kaplan courses to outfox the SAT, take assertiveness courses, work at golf with the concentration of Buddhist monks. Botox and tanning salons help when you're pressed for time. Your genuine self—your soul—is who you are in the shower at 6 a.m.

Jesse Jackson rightly encouraged young audiences to shout, "I am *some*body!" But that confident battle cry is legitimate only if one *acts* like a somebody. Humanity invites us to evolve beyond our simian forebears, but we never leave our natural animal inertia behind. It's always inside, trying to drag us back down, to resist challenge, to squirm our way through. Therefore, anyone who claims to be adult (as opposed to just "grown-up") ought to be demonstrably more confident than when we left school, with a superego stripped of everything not validated by objective reality, a *character*, personally forged and accepted.

Character—self-esteem, which refuses to demean itself—has need of two seemingly contradictory qualities—vulnerability and rigor: spine. On the one hand, you have to put down your guard against the truth and other people; on the other hand, you have to commit yourself firmly to what you know to be the truth and be willing to stand up and defend what you believe.

Vulnerability is essential to human growth. If humanity rises above animality in that you can know, and love, and grow *more* human, then there have to be *better* answers than the ones you've had so far, *more* people you can love, and on a consistently deeper level. To become more humanized, you have to be *humble* before the truth, wherever it leads, humble before the other person, who can open deeper levels of his or her self to you—and in so doing open deeper levels of your self, too. But to be humble, you must have some kind of confidence in your own self.

Commitment—spine—is also essential to the formation of character. If you stand for everything, you stand for nothing. Yet, especially nowadays when "things" change so often and rapidly, most of us balk at commitment, preferring to "keep an open mind"—in case something better comes along—not wanting to be considered pig-headed or old-fashioned, not realizing the most open mind is an empty head. Until we say, "thus far; no further," we are walking reactions to other people's choices: a personality without character.

On the other hand, perhaps the major pitfall of getting older is the utterly unfounded belief that we have at least most of the answers. (Google the poem "Ozymandias.") If experience has taught us anything, it should be that we will always have more to learn than we've learned.

Once we reason our way to an opinion (not just mull it over, but gather the evidence, sift it, draw a conclusion), then we have to stand up and defend it—no matter what anyone else says. If "they" offer substantial and just criticism, then we go back and work the opinion over and try it out again. Having a personality is inevitable; having character takes work.

Sharks and tigers never suffer doubt. Only humans do. Like genuine guilt, genuine doubt is a healthy hunch things aren't as right as they should be, that ideas we've been content with so far need retuning—or perhaps complete rethinking. That holds true even regarding truths that we've felt comfortably *certain* about since we left school—and since then have never submitted to honest adult scrutiny, accepted as unchallengeable on evidence slimmer than we'd now accept before buying a car. No problem with that—as long as you do sit down now and figure out a better answer. It's what we were born for. It's called evolution.

The Insatiable Restlessness

A high school senior once asked the best question I've heard in class in fifty years: "Why is fulfillment always in the future?" Every human—from the lowest serf to Alexander the Great—felt that itch: "There's gotta be *more!*" The Stones got it right: "I can't get no satisfaction." It's that human discontent that led to agriculture when some smart woman said, "I'm sick of foraging out in the woods. I'm gonna stick stuff in the ground right here at my door." It gradually led us out of the caves, into villages and cities, over the mountains and out onto the unpredictable seas. It created pots, symbols, literacy, weapons, and ultimately telescopes and microscopes and oscilloscopes and proctoscopes. And along the way, it kept asking, "What are we here for? What will make us *happy?* What do the gods want of us? When will we get '*there*'?"

Well. Now you *are* there. You've got a far better perspective on life from what you had when you left school behind. The human hunger you feel now is almost surely quite different from "way back when." When we left schooling, we had to focus pretty unswervingly on making a living, no matter how our teachers and professors had insisted on learning what living is *for*.

That hunger for "more" had to concentrate on matters that might not have been more *important* but were surely more *pressing*. Satisfying (impressing) a boss, making more money to take care of far wider concerns, dealing with battalions of problems like mortgages, tuitions, spouses-children-colleagues-clients-neighbors with minds (and agendas) of their own.

But now, we're at least supposed to have "arrived." More or less, we have the leisure to gather together the evidence and, rather than merely *being* drifted toward an end of life here, we can become friends with this person with whom we've been sharing a skin—and a lot of laughs and tears and love—all these years. Otherwise, your soul is no more than a neighbor who's lived on the other side of the impenetrable apartment wall. It was the wisdom inscribed over the portal to the Oracle of Delphi: *Gnothi Seauton*, "Know Thyself." It's why you were made different.

Time to go "back to school" and discover what you've really learned along the way.

God wrote the answers to those nifty questions about fulfillment, I think, right into the way we're made. What separates us from other animals is that we can understand and love. Other animals can know brute facts, but none we know of asks why. Other animals can give their lives for their own young, but only we can give our lives—often without dying—even for people we don't *like* at the moment. Ask any teacher or parent.

What will make us, at least for the moment, fulfilled? I suspect it's contentment to *keep* asking questions—without hankering for definitive, final answers, grateful we'll never run out of *terras incognitas* to explore. And I suspect success is also rooted in confident serenity to be attentively aware of clues in the faces of everyone around us, as *alert* as a new mother is to the wordless signals from her newborn child. That watchfulness—that continual sensitizing of the mind and heart—is demanding, often without palpable rewards, often fatiguing.

But it sure beats dying before we die.

What God Expects

Over and above the invitation of humanity, Christians believe they've also been invited to share in the life of the Trinity. We at least *claim* to be adopted sons and daughters of the superalive God. I doubt, though, you've pondered that idea much, decompacted it so the content would shock the hell out of you (literally). Moreover, it should shock the life *into* you: the divine life, which all those religious teachers called "grace"—and almost surely hadn't the slightest idea what they were talking about. As I remember it, the content of "grace" was sort of like Antabuse, the drug alcoholics take to make them nauseous if they take a drink. In what turned into twenty-eight years of formal Catholic education, I can't remember *anyone* saying grace should make me more lively, more bumptious, more contagiously happy than people who lacked it.

All I remember is rules. And safeguards. And warnings. (And of course hell, although that now seems to have flamed out.) Most who've wandered from the church seem to remember it the same way. So do many of the thousands of kids I've taught for the last half-century: rules.

More than a few have suggested that, once the Christian community felt free to come out of the catacombs, and the gospel became not only legitimate but expected, and the vastness of the Roman Empire required literate managers, and the literate clergy (clericals) easily slipped into positions of influence and power (and into the mansions and costumes of the wealthy), a profound seismic shift occurred ever so gradually in the church. (See Dostoevsky, *The Grand Inquisitor*.)

At first even Gentile Christians lived radically the same way as Jesus and the first apostles and disciples—lower class, hunted, despised, and yet shockingly indifferent to entry qualifications ("There is no longer Jew nor Greek, slave nor free, male and female; for all of you are one in Christ Jesus." [Galatians 3:28]), and they were also shockingly kind even to those who sought to kill them. Although Jesus respected the law, he was not above accommodation and adaptability, and they were too busy anyway baptizing new recruits and scuttling into hiding places to be overly fastidious about bylaws, canonized requirements, background checks. No need for collections to enhance their underground places of worship.

But some still-curious Catholics are tempted to consider the unnerving possibility that ever-so-slowly "The New Pharisees" took over. Niceties of doctrine—in those years when all Christians from pope to barkeep were feeling their way around Christian understanding—became the cause not only of academic wordplay but cobblestone battles in the streets over precisions that today are now safely locked away in the Creed—which no sane adult Christian now cares to parse. "Leave the thinking to the officers and horses; they have bigger heads." Pay, pray, and obey.

The head edged out the heart. Fear outdrew love. Guilt was easier to sell than friendship.

And there matters held for thousands of years, until our very own time. Surely the Mystique of Sin held sway at St. John's Grammar School in the 1930s and 1940s, and in my four years at a Jesuit high school. In my first two years at Holy Cross College, we memorized the catechism (again) and recited it weekly. It was, in effect, a seminary for lay apostles, and I confess I loved it and still miss its (unjustified) bulwark certitude and freedom from disquietude, the deeply felt sense of unquestioned fellowship and passive conviction. Then, along came the peasant dumpling John XXIII and invited the villagers into the ivory theological tower.

The analogy is much too reductionist, but it's tempting to draw a very rough parallel between the Catholic shift since Vatican II (*after*, for most of us, our Catholic education had been "wrapped up") and the tectonic shift in Judaism between the message of John the Baptist and the message of Jesus. And even that shift was more profound than our religion teachers saw. There's more than a little truth in claiming that Catholicism back then was more comfortable with Old Testament righteousness than with New Testament superaliveness and joy.

John himself said, "I baptize with water: he will baptize with the Holy Spirit and fire." I'll bet no teacher or homilist drew your attention to the radical differences between water and fire.

John—and the Old Testament, and the Pharisees, and the Catholic teaching I grew up with—was almost exclusively about cleansing from sin. But Jesus was about setting ablaze, energizing, soaring beyond justice to fierce concern. Making us discontent even with "mere" virtue, empathy, kindness. "I'll not stop at sharing my excess with you. I'll write letters to those who hold the common purse and decide how my taxes are spent. Almost certainly, those letters will effect no more change in the world of the disinherited than one unwanted sweater or pair of gloves. But no matter what, there's a change in me. I'll have forced my concern beyond the stifling cocoon of my own need to be effective. Even if the time it took to write the letter meant I had to miss a rerun of *Two and a Half Men.*"

Another aspect of Jesus no one imposed on me while they smothered me with Jesus-Meek-and-Mild: they ignored the Jesus in the gospels who always went *looking* for trouble! They didn't execute him because he just wanted everybody to "make nice." First of all, he refused to shut up! And he refused to back down on his claim he'd been chosen. And he was constantly on the prowl for do-overs: whores, crooks, lepers, the demonized, the rule mongers. He kept *provoking* debates with the know-it-alls. Didn't he even *consider* that a cure on the *next* day would be just as welcome to the victim as on the Sabbath—and there'd be no fuss from the clergy?

Fortunately for him, he didn't have to face "the slings and arrows of outrageous fortune" for more than thirty years or so. Which misses his lesson to his friends: Whatever time he did have, Jesus used every second to (forgive me) kick butt!

Every second of your golden years is a golden second.

It's astonishing how one's world explodes once we're tempted outside our need for security. Otherwise, it's like having wings and scorning flight. Our Catholic learning was so well intentioned— and so crippling. Maybe we're at a time of life when we might read a bit and get more than a child's idea of God. And ourselves. Anthony DeMello pictures God saying to someone praying, "I am so pleased with you, so grateful." Like most of us, the one praying protests; how could God be grateful to a wretch like me? But God says, "Surely you would be grateful beyond words to anyone who did for you even a small part of what you've done for Me. Do you think I have less of a heart than you?"

The heresy of Pelagianism prays that "we may *merit* to be co-heirs to eternal life." Can we become mature enough to grasp that Jesus already *did* that *for* us? That all we have to do is step forward and claim it? That it's impossible for us to merit what we already have?

If this book has a challenge, this is it: "Are you humble enough to submit to believing God considers *you* worth his Son's death?"

There you have it: Christianity broken open to the core.

Surprised?

2.
Attitude

There is a fountain of youth: it's your mind—
your talents, the creativity you bring to your life
and the lives of people you love. When you learn
to tap this source, you'll truly have defeated age.

—Sophia Loren

Just to stir up the sludge, I begin every class with a ten-statement survey—agree/disagree—just to see where the public-to-be-cajoled stands. One says, "The law of self-preservation is the most basic drive of specifically human nature." Almost without exception, most agree, which shows how biology teachers have gotten through better than religion teachers.

Before reading further, pause for a moment and try to remember what your idea of "success" was at age twenty. Write it out if it helps. Then, do the same for your idea of success now, after these years of experience. Are the "proofs" of success less concrete, more intangible than they were then? And yet, nonetheless, is your advice to the next generation more focused on job security than on forging a character? "How much can you make doing that?" If your grandson said he'd like to be a priest, would you suggest he see a psychiatrist first?

No denying we're partly animal, but our human nature is an invitation to transcend our animal nature. Even so, there's also no denying that, no matter what our success in domesticating the beast in us, we can never be totally free of the intrusive thing. Even Mother Teresa found her body demanded to eat and sleep, and her kinship with apes and tigers also must have made her snappish every now and then. That self-centered instinct we share with drowning mongrels is what leads us in our weak moments to cheat, to keep silent before intimidation and injustice, to let other sleeping dogs lie. Peace means being unbothered, being content with—or at least resigned to—the status quo, being incurious, being tenuously secure.

In fact, loveless cohabitation of the soul with the beast is a pretty good explanation for me of what we've always described as original sin—which, as we all know by now, even baptism doesn't nullify.

At its most extreme, that *fear* of suffering is—with heavy irony—the very cause of the worst of sufferings. Could the Nazi extermination camps have existed without the gut fear in the SS functionaries who did the scut work that they'd go to the Russian front if they refused? Could they have succeeded if prisoners corralled in ghettoes hadn't said to themselves that conforming was better than being shot? Better a live slave than a dead lion.

In his book *Man's Search for Meaning,* Viktor Frankl, a psychiatrist who survived the camps, asks whether the prisoner was responsible for his situation in that ghastly nightmare world. And his answer is, "Yes." The prisoner wasn't responsible for being trapped in an unmerited hell. But he or she was responsible for the ultimate freedom: the freedom to choose one's *attitude* in the face of adversity. "Here lies the chance," Frankl says, "for a man either to make use of or to forgo the opportunities of attaining the moral values that a difficult situation may afford him. And this decides whether he is worthy of his sufferings or not."

If you've ever worked in a hospital or visited a retirement home, you've seen a radical difference in attitudes in the patients. Some react to unmerited suffering with anger. Some are bitter. Others whine. But there are always a gallant few who intimidate by their resolute resilience.

Remember the Andrews Sisters: "Ya gotta accentuate the positive, eliminate the negative." Whenever I feel tempted to immature emotional responses—anger or just brooding on "the unfairness of things"—I want to regrab the down-to-earth advice of the wonderful flinty nuns from my past about sexual temptations: "*Distract* yourself! Sing! If you have to, cup your hands over your ears and paddle them and say in your head, 'I'm not *listening* to you!'" Now that such temptations no longer have such easy access into my barnacled old soul, I find that advice still remarkably sound. Whenever I hear the remotest siren song to self-pity—even brooding too much on my self—I run in the other direction, to salvific distractions.

Thus, I've made a vow to myself, I will never—ever, *ever*—ask myself, "How am I doin'?" I'm still alive, dammit! That's the most important gift I still have. That's "Probably better'n I deserve"— because I did absolutely nothing to deserve being here or waking up this morning. What I still have is sure worth more than what I'm missing.

One very salutary effect, when "the days dwindle down to a precious few," *should* be that each day is worth immeasurably more than it was when we were seventeen. Because we are!

Jesus offers the same advice: "Don't let them intimidate you! Don't fear those who deprive the body of life but can't destroy the soul" (Matthew 10:28). The fiends who administered the Nazi camps could degrade the bodies of the inmates, but they couldn't touch their souls—if the inmates refused to surrender them.

Personally, I find that insight very, very intimidating, especially when I'm the victim of my *own* intimidations, my *own* overbearing moods, my *own* surrender to creeping self-pity. Something quite self-deceptive in me really enjoys playing Hamlet, posturing to an enthralled audience of one over my own heroic anguish. Something both sane and redeemed in me keeps whispering, "Oh, Hamlet, for God's sake, will you get on with it? Doesn't this self-loathing get a bit boring?" At my age, I should know better.

Strange, no? In those moments, self-*preservation* actually dictates self-*denial* to any reasonable person. If you want to find yourself, lose yourself. Striding confidently is an act of your faith, made manifest and empowering.

If you want to be happy, shuck off the resentments, the grudges, the slavery to what you guess are other people's opinions. If you want to stop drowning, let go of the anchor.

3.
My Soul = Who I Am

It's my world that I want to have a little pride in
My world and it's not a place I have to hide in
Life's not worth a damn
Till you can say, hey world, I am what I am.
— *La Cage au Folles*

At some cutting-edge prestigious university like Southern Cal, they're doing studies of people's auras. Those neuroexperts say they can detect an emanation from the body on special cameras and film. Everyone has unique intensities, colors, moods. Almost like taking a picture of your soul. Maybe the artists who painted those big golden frisbees on the back of saints' heads weren't so far off after all. As Hamlet says, "There are more things in heaven and earth, Horatio, than are dreamt of in your philosophy." Or your physics or your theology, for that matter. All those realities that are true and real and humanizing but that elude empirical traps.

The burden of this chapter is to ask whether one's aura—one's soul—has to start fading with age. Or can one's attitude keep it pulsing, intensifying? How much more experience do we have now to stoke our auras with than when we were kids?

Humbling—therefore liberating—to realize the limits of both our vision and our understanding. How could anyone, even as knowing about astronomy as Galileo, have conceived a universe enormous beyond our power to imagine, where galaxies have millions of suns that make our sun look like a firefly? How could anyone, even as steeped in genetics as Gregor Mendel, have imagined we'd decipher strings of DNA and restructure our own bodies? How could anyone, even as skilled an engineer as Edison, have predicted we'd one day routinely sit at machines with forty book-length manuscripts in their electronic memories?

At this very moment, we're each being skewered by neutrinos—with no discernible mass, no electric charge, slicing through the whole earth without being slowed down. Every time we bite a burger, a zillion unseen agents in our bodies fire up to process it—without our permission. Consider the miracles of our eyes: two jellied cameras with bellows and lenses, taking color pictures eighteen hours a day—and you never have to change the film. Then our minds change those pictures into abstract ideas. As St. Exupery said, "The essential is always invisible."

Like our souls.

At the transfiguration, the godliness in Jesus' soul burned through the surfaces of what we mistakenly believe are the limits of what's real, what Eastern religions call *maya*, illusion. Science has exactly the same insight. The chairs you're sitting in right now only *appear* solid. Actually, they're buzzing swarms of molecules and electrons moving so fast that they *seem* at rest. And most of it's empty space! If you compressed all that's truly solid in each chair, it would take up less space than a pinpoint. Ah, but the energy compressed into that tiny space!

Gerard Manley Hopkins, the Jesuit poet, put it as well as anyone: "The world is charged with the grandeur of God, / It will flame out, like shining from shook foil. . . . / Oh, morning, at the brown brink eastward springs— / Because the Holy Ghost over the bent / World broods with warm breast and with ah! bright wings." Only a few are graced to be aware of those pulsations.

There you see the abyss between the "world" as we ordinarily use the word, and the way Jesus used it. "The World" he saw in contrast to the Kingdom, we now call "The System" or the deified "Economy" whose values seem to nearly all of us—even veteran Catholics—unquestionable.

We accept a world addicted to surfaces, where the essential is only the visible, tangible, marketable. We're mesmerized by surfaces: jewelry, complexion, hair, clothes, bodies. Image outweighs substance, personality trumps character, notoriety beats genuine achievement. The late-night talk shows are proof nothing succeeds like the appearance of success.

Coming to Christ with more to offer than we had fifty years ago—deeper wisdom honed by abrasions of harsh experience— takes more reflection than many of us have had time to give it. As

Richard Rohr writes so incisively in *Falling Upward: A Spirituality for the Two Halves of Life,*

> It takes a huge push, much self-doubt, and some degree of separation for people to find their own soul and their own destiny apart from what Mom and Dad always wanted them to be and do. To move beyond family-of-origin stuff, local church stuff, cultural stuff, flag-and-country stuff is a path few of us follow positively and with integrity. The pull is just too great, and the loyal soldier fills us with appropriate guilt, shame, and self-doubt, which . . . feels like the very voice of God.

Most of our lives, well-meaning folks told us the purpose of life is "to find God's plan," like a kind of syllabus or more likely a scripted play with a recognizable plot line. Nice try. Just one more excuse to get trapped in our metaphors, as we do when we talk of old Adam and Eve incurring some kind of unpayable *debt* to God that even industrial Clorox can't bleach away.

Psst! Life isn't a play, with a plot line and stage directions. Anybody over eighteen should have realized the "Director" (God) keeps shoving onstage with surprises that totally upset and reroute the plot. He sends unscheduled bosses, colleagues, and hurricanes in from the wings—always just when "happily ever after" looks like a sure thing. No one can claim adulthood until he or she yields to the inescapable fact that there is *no* plot (except an endlessly unfolding one)—that it's all *improvisation.* That's what we accept when we accept "God's plan"! That our Creator, after a while, dislikes *stasis,* routine, complacency. His "plan" has managed to discard 99 percent of the species he's made; evolution keeps rolling along; and, as the great prophet Bob Dylan wrote, "He not busy being born is busy dying."

Life's not a play. It's a *journey.* And what you bring to that unpredictable challenge is you—your soul, your Who-I-Am—which was born to welcome the unexpected as a way of intensifying that self. Our Lady said it: "Be it done unto me according to your word." So that she could then say, "My soul *magnifies* the Lord." That's what St. Ignatius Loyola meant when he said we're here for "the *greater* glory of God." We'll encounter him every step of the way—even in the monsters, and swamps, and nasty checkout girls. The unexpected is God, in disguise.

As we hear, again from Hamlet, who lacked the quality entirely, "Readiness is all." We're not here to "arrive," to "achieve," to "win." We're here as pilgrims equipped with wits, if we choose to develop and use them. Tennyson caught it in "Ulysses": "To strive, to seek, to find, and not to yield." In the going, we're already there.

Eastern mystics call the individual soul Atman, the divine spark within each of us that hungers for union with the Ultimate Being. And Rilke said,

Ah, Night! Bursting with new-born stars
strewing pathways of fire as they soar
in silent pilgrimage through endless space,
and I stand smallened by their hugeness.
And yet within me, deeply rooted, is a light
already safe at home and never to be dimmed.
(translation mine)

Despite our quite different training, we Christians also crave electric contact with that fiery reality who coruscates under all the surfaces. If only we had the time to pull aside and rest awhile, away from the busyness, the distractions, the surfaces. We might see the auras surrounding those we love—and those we don't. We might be able to sense our own auras, our own souls. We might be able to reach with our souls into the heart of things and find God there.

My soul—my truest, deepest self—holds all the other parts of "me" together: body, mind, memories, convictions. My soul is my integrity. It's often self-doubting, too timid, so easily diverted. Unless I take hold of my soul, the "I" of me will be enslaved to uncountable contradictory voices from the commercials, neighbors, church, even my long-dead parents. Like a shattered mirror, reflecting every influence of my life. Except me.

And all the while, like a great underground river of fire and light, God passes me by.

4.

Staying Hungry

And what fool would crave all the gold, all the power, all the flattery in the world at cost of being wretched inside, unsatisfied, frustrated because you can't have the impossible? Then you die. Unless you live the life God sends, you'll have no life at all.

—Mark 8:34–37 (translation mine)

When John the Baptist generously sends the very first disciples off to catch up with Jesus (John 1:29–34), Jesus asks them the *one* question none of my teachers, in twenty-eight years of formal education, ever asked me. Not a *single one*: "What are you looking for?"

Take a dog for a walk, endlessly curious, stopping to sniff for no reason we discern. And, given all we know about dogs, there's no reason. For them, it's just, "What's next?" Sort of like enduring TV on Friday nights. But we humans are hardwired for a further curiosity beyond just facts—understanding. We're born with the humans-only question: "Why?"

In *Cat's Cradle*, Kurt Vonnegut has a nice little story about the creation in which God kneels in the mud making dolls of everything that will be. Then Mud-as-Man sits up, looks around, and asks his question, very politely: "What is the purpose for all this?" And God says, "Everything must have a purpose?" And Mud-as-Man says, "Of course." And God replies, "Then I leave it to you to think of one for all this." And God walks away.

At the opposite pole is the brilliant microbiologist Richard Dawkins, saying, "We humans have purpose on the brain. We find it hard to look at anything without wondering what it is 'for,' what the motive for it is, or the purpose behind it . . . [when it] is actually random bad luck. But this is just an exaggerated form of a nearly universal delusion."

Odd that a "universal" human quality could be so easily dismissed as irrelevant. And odd that we're the only ones cursed with a hunger for which there's no food.

As soon as little kids discover the magic of words, it's incessant, "Why . . . why . . . why?" And maybe the most fitting question on our deathbeds will be, "Why?" One litmus test of how much the years have wearied away our zest for life is whether we still keep barking back at anything unreasonable, if we're still stubbornly asking, "Okay, but *why*?"

"Why is fulfillment always in the future?" It seems most poor souls are like donkeys with carrots dangling at the end of a stick tied to their heads. They chase and chase and chase. "I Can't Get No Satisfaction!" And Peggy Lee: "Is That All There Is?" And Macbeth: "[Life] is a tale / Told by an idiot, full of sound and fury / Signifying nothing."

Knowing beforehand that we're going to die—and having a lifetime to ponder that inequity—is a really dirty trick. Especially if it's a delusion that a mindless evolution just stumbled into. You can't ask why of a dumb force.

Human beings are the only entities we know who are always discontent. Everything that gratifies us wears out, moves away, finds someone they like better, dies. Victims of the American Dream are forever frustrated, because there's always more, newer, faster. "Highs" from eating, drinking, drugs, sex, never seem to achieve permanence. Its victims become insatiable. The weekend high drifts away, and the alarm clock clangs Monday morning. As soon as you're a big-shot eighth-grader, you're a bum again two months later. Then a senior, then a bum. A senior again, a bum. A manager, but the youngest. Then president. Then you die.

And when you turn sixty, your speedometer refuses to keep up.

"Losing one's soul" doesn't mean falling into hell. It means falling apart. Like a car gradually disintegrating, lacking its internal dynamism and connections, dragging along, till it's just bits and hunks along the highway that other vehicles simply whiz past. Sad, huh?

The difference between a drifter and a pilgrim is that the one is always yearning to achieve satisfaction, and the other's satisfied with striving. The same difference between a sprinter and a marathon runner. Ridiculous time splittings motivate the sprinter; the marathoner is content to run, with almost no chance of "scoring." Chesterton said, poets don't go mad, chess players do. Rationalists, perfectionists, achievers try to cross the infinite sea, thus *forcing* it to become finite. Poets' souls rejoice that the sea is infinite, and there's always more to discover.

Without a mind behind it all, the soul—that universal great hunger—is a cruel scourge. But if God really *is*, then that universal hunger is an invitation—into forever.

The Greek word for "soul" is *psyche*, the root of "psychotherapy," which Freud (a meticulous stylist) did *not* mean as "mind-doctoring" but rather "soul-healing," far more intuitive and interpersonal than rationalist pigeonholing. But even more revealing: *psyche* originally meant "butterfly," a perfect image for the self-emerging bright-winged from the ugly carapace of the cocoon. But as soon as you think you've "arrived"—or even worse that you're "finished"—you're actually worse than dead. Like a butterfly yearning backward to the warmth of the cocoon and mewing, "Do I *still* have to *fly?*"

5.
Perspective

It's paradoxical that the idea of living a long life appeals to everyone, but the idea of getting old doesn't appeal to anyone.

—Andy Rooney

O'Malley's second law is "You'll never go broke betting on dumb." (For enquiring minds, O'Malley's first law is "The less you know, the more certain you can be.") Dumb is a virulent and almost ineradicable strain of the primordial virus called original sin. Ironically, for an agent so destructive, dumb is almost always intimately linked to righteousness (usually self-bestowed). It most often manifests itself in total lack of objectivity and perspective, and it doesn't have any truck with obstacles as vulgar as common sense. Dumb does not "do" nuance. Dumb is what impels otherwise capable men to fly jet planes filled with hundreds of human beings into skyscrapers filled with thousands of other human beings and obliterate them—in the name of Almighty God—which then impels others to launch preemptive war based on insufficient evidence against even more human beings and deprive them of their lives—in the name of the same God, albeit with a less sandblasted personality.

Dumb has nothing whatever to do with IQ or academic degrees. Apparently, Oedipus was the cleverest guy in town, but his perspective was severely cramped. For a while, Hitler was a tactical genius. But short sighted. Many even brilliant people seem to live far more constricted, defensive, joyless lives than they need to.

Like other effects of original sin, dumb isn't eradicated by baptism, nor ordination to priesthood or episcopacy or even papacy—as witness the very first pope who fumbled so often. Also quite a few of his successors, including Roderigo Borgia, Alexander VI, something of the Marquis de Sade with a tiara, had lost all true perspective. Ordination didn't see the inhumanity in the Inquisition, the Crusades, the enslavement of the Americas, the *Syllabus of Errors.*

Sadly—very often tragically—dumb achieves equally lethal potency at the opposite end of the spectrum from corrupt potentates, in the good-hearted nobodies who fall victim to the simplistic mouthing of muddle-headed teachers—whether imams, itinerant retreat givers, demagogues, or televangelists—who relieve simple folk of the insupportable burden of thinking for themselves in the complex world God created, in divine defiance of simplistic bumper-sticker answers.

Literalist gospel study sees wealth as evil (despite weekly collections), true humility as self-hatred, God as the jailer who sells Get Out of Purgatory Free cards. Passages about sheep can be twisted to suggest we be mindlessly submissive to other human beings and not just to Christ, The Shepherd. If you achieve any hard-won eminence, they warn, you're headed for hell (despite the fact the same Jesus told us to shine from the housetops); if you yield to pride in a job well done, you've ingested your own doom (despite the fact the same Jesus told us to develop our talents); if you have money, you're headed for a hopeless encounter with a needle's eye (despite the fact a penniless Samaritan would have had nothing solid to offer the battered victim by his roadside).

That same simplemindedness and enslavement to metaphors still shackles a great many beyond-adulthood Christians. Now, as birthday candles fight for space, might be a time to accept liberation from childish answers, despite all the yada yada we've heard for years from experts. Over all these years, just how much richer is your grasp of the basic beliefs from the time of your last academic submission to religious education?

When I perform a baptism, I can't bring myself to believe this tiny bundle, still incapable of controlling her own excretory habits, can be in any way guilty before the God who created everything *else* in the universe innocent. I can't buy the idea that the God who expects us to forgive seventy times seven times could hold a grudge against all human beings for thirty thousand years solely because one not-too-bright pair of nudists ate just one piece of fictional fruit at the behest of a fast-talking snake. (When did snakes stop talking?) Add to that the prickly message from my left brain where I keep science stuff: if Adam and Eve caused death, what bushwhacked all those dinosaurs whose bones prove they were all dead before any of us came along?

And do I want to worship such a vindictive God, who refused to let us off the hook till his unspeakably holy Son suffered desertion, mockery, condemnation by church and state, spiking to a cross—a punishment so disgraceful it was reserved for traitors and runaway slaves? Who felt so deserted by God that he screamed out on the edge of despair?

Is that conundrum settled by the easy-to-hand, mindless answer: atonement, ransom? No matter how you pretty up the definition, "ransom" is paid only to a *hostile* power, which is not what the Father of the prodigal Son leads us to believe God is in our regard—even after we have sinned and proven ourselves deserving of God's displeasure.

Suffering and sin are absolutely inevitable. Without them, we'd never be humble enough to realize how lucky we are—to be here at all, how grateful we should be. (So many people never come to that, as if they'd done something to deserve an invitation.) Why was the sinless Jesus baptized? Why did he die such an awful death?

To show us how being human is done—with trust. And dignity.

Maybe Jesus was baptized for a reason having nothing to do with unworthiness: to offer a lesson about being fully human. Of course, every one of us is born human simply because we had demonstrably human parents. But—unlike the nature of any other species—human nature is only *potential*. It needn't be activated just because we're born with it—as witness pimps, pushers, and more-refined exploiters.

At his baptism, Jesus showed that, by being born human we're born *prone* to weakness, to temptations no other species has—choosing the easier way, even if it's bad. Then he proved that, immediately after his baptism, actually facing temptations in the desert. Because he was human.

From the outset, the gospels surrender to the truth, the way things really are, the will of God. Our Lady submitted, even if the task proposed to her was beyond reason. Joseph yielded and took her to wife against all reason. God's Son, at the incarnation, St. Paul says, *"sese exinanivit,"* emptied himself—he freely surrendered all the perquisites of being God, in order to fulfill the will of his Father, to struggle with being human, incomplete, tormented by doubts, subservient to a God who far too often doesn't *seem* to know the enormity of what he's asking.

Jesus' submission to baptism embodies who humans are: sons and daughters of God—yet, prone to the delusion that, because we're so enormously gifted, in ways no other creatures are, we don't need to rely on God. Adam and Eve's sin may not have happened at the start of time. But it happens *all* the time, every day. It's the only doctrine we can prove from the daily papers.

At his baptism and at his death, Jesus said, "Don't be afraid. Watch me. When you do like this, you'll hear God telling you who you truly are: 'You are mine. And I'm well pleased.'"

In *The Screwtape Letters*, a supervisor demon advises his apprentice out in the field that he needn't make his clients serial killers or purveyors of porn. Corrupting the good is far easier than that. All you have to do is give the chumps a mirror. Then, whether they're mesmerized by their own fatal charms or their fatal flaws, they're immobilized, neutralized, of no help or harm to anyone. One way or the other, whether the victim is self-aggrandized or self-debased—either way, they feel they're number one. The process is diabolically simple and almost unfailingly effective, because it disguises itself as virtue: arrogant humility.

Jesus, our model, honestly accepted who he was and defied simplistic teachers. When he offered a child as his answer, he meant adults like us should be childlike, not childish, that is, "seen but not heard." He did say we were to be as guileless as doves but also shrewd as serpents. I like to think he did mean us to regain the wonderment of children, the lack of skepticism that lets them run open-armed to strangers, the exuberance that sees a castle in a discarded box and a fairy godmother in a bedraggled mop wringer. (Like Carol Burnett, whose real-life challenges have clearly forged her soul into a deep leaden keel to weather storms that would capsize flat bottoms.)

But the Jesus who shadowboxed the Pharisees so often, twisted their perverted logic back onto them, blasted them as "hypocrites" (and worse) was no goo-goo-eyed naïf. I suspect he'd probably shake the stuffing out of most of us who aren't speechlessly grateful for the gifts he's given each of us to improve the lives of everybody around us.

Poverty doesn't automatically engender virtue, and wisdom doesn't come automatically from old age. Only gray hair and wrinkles.

6.
The Fifth Dimension

REBECCA: *I never told you about that letter Jane Crofut got from her minister when she was sick. He wrote Jane a letter and on the envelope the address was like this: It said: Jane Crofut; The Crofut Farm; Grover's Corners; Sutton County; New Hampshire; United States of America.*
GEORGE: *What's funny about that?*
REBECCA: *But listen, it's not finished: the United States of America; Continent of North America; Western Hemisphere; the Earth; the Solar System; the Universe; the Mind of God—that's what it said on the envelope.*
GEORGE: *What do you know!*
REBECCA: *And the postman brought it just the same.*
GEORGE: *What do you know!*
—Thornton Wilder, *Our Town*

Rebecca's insight puts Jane into *context*—against a background, yardstick, matrix—by which to assess her place in "the scheme of things," her *value*. Confederate money is relatively valueless now because it's lost its context: the Confederate States of America. In Nazi Germany, Jews and Slavs were *Untermenchen*, "less than human," not because of their inner, objective lesser worth but because of Hitler's arbitrary designation—backed by the Gestapo and S.S.

When we amble along into "The Golden Age," there's always the temptation to believe our currency is devalued when our purchasing power—and our ability to provoke more than token respect—has shifted noticeably.

Picture a little girl like Jane or Rebecca with a $50 bill in one fist and a teddy bear in the other. There are three very distinct values in that picture: the money, the doll, and the girl. The money has economic power, a real value. The teddy bear has little or no value to strictly objective, rational observers—but a real-if-intangible value to the little girl (and to any observer with greater sensitivity than a tax assessor). And within the little girl herself resides a truly real-if-unquantifiable value (no matter what Hitler asserted or how much power he had to enforce it).

Another evaluative context (especially in a world that discounts "the Mind of God" in Jane's minister's address) is size: how much land you can acquire (like antebellum plantations or Axis rule over all Europe, North Africa, and a lot of the Pacific) or, by extension, one's bank balance, dynasty, awards cabinet, framed book covers, newspaper clippings. Given the inescapable fact of death, however, the value denoted by those accumulations is fragile and fleeting. There are no U-hauls on hearses.

Which calls in question the reliability of many yardsticks.

In a telephone booth (if any still exist), you look substantially more significant than standing next to the Sears Tower. Expanding the contextual focus to all of Chicago, you diminish to hardly a squeak. Stretch that background even further to a map of the United States, you become inconsequential. But keep going—to an earthrise from the moon. Pull back gradually further and further, like the *Journey to the Stars* film on the ceiling of the Hayden Planetarium. Expand your context to the entire solar system, then the staggering extent of the Milky Way galaxy. Even at the speed of light, it would take 100,000 years to cross it. The light from some of its stars that we see on a given night began its travel through space before there were humans. Quite possibly the source of that light already died and is no longer "there." But the light it sent hurtling out still is.

Keep going. Out into the unmappable expanse that encompasses hundreds of billions of galaxies (try to grapple with that), each one at least as large as our own tidy neighborhood Milky Way galaxy, which is a mere 100,000 times six trillion miles in diameter.

On that intimidating map, find yourself. Even if you live to a hundred.

And it gets worse.

Really savvy astrophysicists like Stephen Hawking now speculate that, despite our past arrogant limitations of reality to backgrounds in which humans are the central focus, that measure is, unthinkably, even *larger*! Hawking suggests this present nearly infinite physical universe could well be merely a castoff from an infinite *series* of universes! Oh, my.

If you don't make a squeak from a map of Chicago, what kind of receiver could capture even a ninety-year endless cater-wauling from you at the far end of an infinite series of physical universes? Less significant, meaningful, consequential—valuable—than the wake of a very tiny ship or a suppressed burp in a cosmic hurricane.

Something ungovernable within me resists being that utterly negligible. Jesse Jackson said it for me: "I am *some*body!"

To see a World in a Grain of Sand
And a Heaven in a Wild Flower,
Hold Infinity in the palm of your hand
And Eternity in an hour.
—William Blake

But wait. What reason is there to restrict reality even to an infinite series of physical universes? "Is that all there is?" If Hawking can dream up his infinite universes, why must I be hesitant to voice my trust that there's a dimension to reality even "larger" than that? What if there were a "beyonder beyond"? The *Really* Real? An Infinite Being Behind It All and a hugely more intense way of existence than material being? "The Mind of God."

Is our suspicion of transcendence—the "other worldly," a humans-only *delusion*? Is it just as childish as what Dawkins calls the almost universal human delusion about purposefulness? When we stand gazing in awe at a star-strewn summer sky and mutter, helplessly, "Oh, my God!" is that simply a reaction of the primitive savage (or the child) still rooted in us after all these years of careful sophistication? When we're transfixed by the power of a storm-savaged beach, the first crocus every spring, an infant's perfect tiny fingernails clutched around just one of our pinkie fingers? One more delusion we really ought to shuck early in adulthood, along with "I disobeyed my parents seven times"? Is awe and wonder an embarrassment one dumps with all due speed the instant puberty clicks on? For fifty years, I've taught a *lot* of young people who think so.

The first sentence of Carl Sagan's *Cosmos* asserts, "The cosmos [the physical universe—the three dimensions of space plus time] is all there is and all there ever was and all there ever will be." What right do even such scientific geniuses as Hawking and Sagan and Dawkins have to set a limit to what *can* be real? As a result of their deserved scientific eminence—and their opinions uncritically accepted and transmitted by elementary, secondary, and college instructors in every field—the young I have reached out to for the last fifty years are more and more skeptical of any assertion that isn't approved kosher by empirical scientists—even when they're speaking well beyond their academic expertise.

Forty years ago, a high school senior challenged me: "Do you think *you're* as smart as Carl *Sagan?*" I said, "Nope. But maybe more honest about what I have a right to claim."

And I arrived at that open-mindedness by a very tortuous journey full of pitfalls and tailspins. I had to flee my equally intransigent (falsely reassuring) certitude that all scientists were as sinister servants of Antichrist as Jews, Masons, Protestants, and the Soviet Politburo. Most people my age got that same rock-ribbed certitude drummed relentlessly into us, edging ever so close to "Outside the (Roman Catholic) Church no salvation."

But then, ever so slowly, many Catholics became less defensive, more accepting—and acceptable. We evolved from immigrant outsiders at the turn of the twentieth century through enthusiastic and mostly uncritical acceptance of American cultural values and attitudes. We willingly improved our socioeconomic status and merged into the mainstream of American secular life. But many "1950s Catholics" still yearn for the consoling uniformity we now sugarcoat with selective memories. The "good old days" weren't really that undilutedly good. We sacrificed a lot of truth back then in the interest of preserving our identity and sense of superiority. (See Mark Massa, S.J., *Catholics and American Culture: Fulton Sheen, Dorothy Day, and the Notre Dame Football Team*, Crossroad, 1999.)

But brilliant naysayers like Sagan, Dawkins, Hitchens, who ridicule a Catholicism now long unlamentedly lost, quite often seem more apodictic and *ex cathedra* than even the most tight-minded popes ever dared to be.

This empiricist bullheadedness about the impossibility (therefore, acceptability and even relevance) of transcendence contradicts empiricists' own inflexible demand for flawless objectivity assessing the evidence, brutal rejection of all prior prejudices intruding on the evaluation process. Yet part of their exacting objectivity requires basic disdain for anthropocentrism, that is, a prejudgment that humanity is the ultimate "goal" of the evolutionary process. How can there be a "goal," they insist, when—from the outset—they've eliminated even a *possibility* of a Designer?

The brightest exemplars of empiricism bar from all assessments, not only God, but any evidence within the human species that would even hint that humans are anything but more complex animals, apes with implanted computers. Thus, no element can intrude on context, on assessment of anything's value, which is not rooted in the *physical* body or brain. Instead, they leave the constitutively human values out of consideration entirely: altruism, honor, forgiveness, hope, compassion even for those we detest, and above all—the need for a *reason to keep going*. As the great agnostic Albert Camus said in his essay *An Absurd Reasoning*,

> There is but one truly serious philosophical problem, and that is suicide. Judging whether life is or is not worth living amounts to answering the fundamental question of philosophy.

Summary exclusion of both God and all the specifically human virtues, which even atheists want in their children, strikes me as the most arrant form of reductionism—omitting essential evidence from consideration of whether life is worthy—because it spoils one's governing theory. Like southern planters and Hitler negating the evident humanity of "inferior races."

Such a refusal of even a *possible* beyond-physical reality also seems rudely anti-intellectual, in clear conflict with the vital imaginative unrest at the heart of all learning, especially science. Isn't it self-defeating to go in search of anything—an unknown planet, the cure for cancer, an element not yet resting in its ready-for-

occupancy slot in the periodic table—with the adamant assertion that the planet or the cure or the new element can't be
found because it *can't* exist?

On the contrary, scientists delight in playing "what if?"
What if we put two lenses in a tube that would enlarge planets incredibly far away or particles incredibly tiny? What if we
fiddled with this yucky bread mold and came up with maybe
a medicine we can call "penicillin"? What if we zapped these
silicon chips?

Then, why not "What if there *were* an entity faster than light?
It'd be moving so fast it would be everywhere at once. (Like
God.) It would be so hyperenergized, it would be at rest. (Like
God.) Science is an arena of search in which the best minds
can accommodate positrons that are electrons with the "wrong"
charge, antimatter that devours its opposite, electrons that are
both solid pellets and ethereal waves at the same time and that
could—according to the best minds—penetrate a barrier without
displacing any part of it and end up at the far end of a different
universe. (That's not arcane theology. It's "hard science.")

Now that superfast entity might be just a mindless impetus,
which is about the best an empiricist can tolerate, a thing (like the
"force" of gravity or the "impulse" of evolution). Sagan uses that
unjustified personification when he writes, "One day, quite by accident, a molecule discovered a way to make crude copies of itself"
and "DNA knows." Brainless molecules can't "discover" anything,
nor can mindless double helixes "know" anything.

Even the unchallenged shibboleth "natural selection" is a
misuse of words in a godless, mindless universe, since "select"
demands the prior cognitional power to envision various options and the volitional power to choose among them. As soon
as you even use the words "Mother Nature," you're on the slippery slope to God. Either the Ultimate Being is *in some way*
personal and purposive—some*one*, not some*thing*—to whom I
owe gratitude for the chance to live—or if not, then as Flannery
O'Connor said about a merely "symbolic" Eucharist, "T'hell
with It."

I feel no need to kiss the floor each morning to thank the Force of Gravity for not losing interest in me overnight and letting me drift out the window into the cold of space. Nor did I feel an urge to comply with the demand of Evolution that I continue the race. Unlike evolution's other products, I exercise my freedom to say "No" to my hardwiring. Evidence strongly suggests that I am—by God—not merely a "rational animal"; I have a context that defies the four dimensions of space/time.

But then along comes Jesus. If I believe the truths that cluster around the person of Jesus Christ, I'm compelled to accept the exalting/humbling belief that I—the once-redheaded son of Bea and Bill O'Malley, a kid from Buffalo, NY, who did very, very poorly at Thomistic metaphysics in Latin—despite all that minimal qualification—have been gratuitously chosen to be a Peer of the Endless Reality-Realm of the Only-Begotten Son of the Most High God. I have been invited into intimate familial friendship with the savior of all humankind, his Father, and their Spirit.

St. Teresa of Avila captured Christ's alchemy of our unworthiness:

> The soul of the just person is a paradise, in which, God tells us, He takes His delight. What do you imagine must that dwelling be in which a King so mighty, so wise, and so pure, containing in Himself all good, can delight to rest? Nothing can be compared to the great beauty and capabilities of a soul; however keen our intellects may be, they are as unable to comprehend them as to comprehend God, for, as He told us, He created us in his own image and likeness.

If you felt beneath significance in an infinite series of universes, little wonder if you feel unworthy of incorporation into such immensity. But you're welcomed not because you deserve inclusion, but because the God who can do anything *wants* to include *you*. He exalts the humble. He's been doing it since he first turned nothing into everything.

But once you situate yourself "out here," in The Really Real, your only choice is to submit gracefully and gratefully. While you're tempted out into this hugeness, like a butterfly distrustful of what's outside the cocoon, look around a bit at your "new" context. You've been here all along, of course, like Helen Keller in the sunshine. If your awareness has been cramped for a long time to the limits of a catechism, it'll take some getting used to. Annie Dillard has a few suggestions about how to start.

There is no less holiness at this time—as you are reading this—than there was on the day the Red Sea parted, or that day in the 30th year, in the 4th month, on the 5th day of the month as Ezekiel was a captive by the river Cheban, when the heavens opened and he saw visions of god. There is no whit less enlightenment under the tree at the end of your street than there was under Buddha's bo tree. . . . In any instant the sacred may wipe you with its finger. In any instant the bush may flare, your feet may rise, or you may see a bunch of souls in trees.

Try to remember all those stories we were told about the gods on Olympus—the beings the Greeks called "The Immortals." Have you ever paused to realize, if you claim to believe (truly, *truly*) that Jesus Christ rose to share resurrection with us, that *you* are one of those: an immortal?

I'm guessing you never did. The "god" I worshiped for half my eighty-plus years was the one who thunders, "For I the Lord thy God am a jealous God, visiting the iniquity of the fathers upon the children unto the third and fourth generation!" (Exodus 20:5 KJV). God sat with an enormous ledger and ink-stained fingers at the top of my tightrope, just waiting for a single false step.

If you had allowed yourself to be accepted and loved by the father of the prodigal, it would be obvious, wouldn't it, in the way you treat people? And carry yourself?

If you still fear death, that's at the very least a hairline crack in your faith. As 1 John says, "There is no fear in love, but perfect love casts out fear; for fear has to do with punishment, and whoever fears has not reached perfection in love" (4:18). "Fear of the Lord" isn't terror. It's *awe*. "That from this great big world, You've chosen me!"

If you genuinely believe that, then death isn't a period. Merely a comma. You are immortal. Right here and now. Eternity is your context.

7.

The Joy of Imperfection

When Simon saw the astonishing harvest of fish that had come into their hands, he fell down at Jesus' knees, and pleaded, "Teacher, you'd best not waste your time with me. I'm a sinful man. Leave me. Please." But Jesus stayed.
—Luke 5:8 (translation mine)

When I was about eight, I suffered a trauma that lasted nearly a lifetime. Msgr. Klauder came for dinner and, just before we sat down, asked me where the bathroom was! I was sucker punched! The *bathroom*? A *priest*?

You can see that, at that age—and for quite some time after—I was in no shape to comprehend the incarnation of the utterly holy as a carpenter whose sweat was no more sweet smelling than our garbageman's. Hardly shameful, since my restrictions on what a properly unsullied God could tolerate was shared by many geniuses: deists like Plato, Aristotle, Cicero, Ben Franklin, Jefferson, Goethe, Kant, Voltaire, and Mark Twain—all of whom realized the predictability of all creation demanded an organizing intelligence. But its very perfection precluded anything as soiled as humanity (despite the fact he/she/they created it all).

Deists are usually very fine human beings, but they're not Christians. No shame in that. Neither were Abraham, Isaac, or Jacob. And we have the word of God's Son that they are still present to his Father (Luke 20:38).

Since that radical disenchantment with the monsignor, I became profoundly suspicious of perfection. I just can't work up much veneration for Maria Goretti or Stanislaus Kostka. They were like all those hateful children adults pointed to when they asked, "Why can't you be like *that*?" Like Aloysius Gonzaga who had to peel off the lustful hands of panting damsels like an infestation of wasps. God never graced me with temptations like that. That's the reason I find such affinity with Professor Harold Hill, *The Music Man*, when he sings,

I smile, I grin, when the gal with a touch of sin walks in.
I hope, I pray, for a Hester to win just one more "A"
The sadder-but-wiser girl's the girl for me.

And it heartens me in my many moments of human weakness that Jesus thought enough of well-intentioned fumblers to make one the first pope. Peter flatly, forthrightly declared his unworthiness even to be in Jesus' presence, much less among his select intimates. And all through the gospels and Acts, Peter—model disciple—is consistently, manifestly imperfect.

When Peter tries to prevent his friend from the suicidal journey to Jerusalem, Jesus immediately rounds on him and calls him "you Satan." Like all the others, Peter grasps what Jesus says and does just well enough to get it backward. When Jesus is under arrest and Peter is accused of being one of his followers, Peter denies it, vehemently, with oaths, three times—not to a soldier with a knife at his throat, but to a *waitress*. (But remember, for all his cowardice, he was *there*.) Even after Pentecost, he still stayed stubborn as an anvil about circumcision and the dietary laws. But when Paul's arguments opened his eyes, the first pope humbly, publicly reversed his position on the essentials of the faith. I admire someone honest enough at least to entertain the possibility he might be wrong.

The Son of God was born in *order* to become imperfect, like us, not knowing but believing, trusting. And if that's good enough for God, it's good enough for me. The point is that, somehow (who'd dare to claim they knew *how*?), the infinite God surrendered the powers of God in order to become fully human—no access to divine knowledge, no force fields to protect him from harm, fatigue, shame, degradation, or even death—so that he could learn as we do, step by hesitant step. As Paul says in Philippians (2:6), "He had always the nature of God, but he did not think by force he should remain equal to God. Instead, he *emptied himself*, to become like us." He didn't stop being God, just stopped being protected by perfection.

One of my most difficult tasks as a teacher to kids—who all

have cell phones and have rarely eaten the same dinner twice in a row—is to make them have even the remotest suspicion their lives are going to be royally screwed up. In a recent survey, a stunning 98 percent of college freshmen agreed with the statement, "I'm sure that one day I'll get to where I want to be in life." Yet four out of five aspiring PhD candidates will be disappointed; a whopping eleven in twelve would-be doctors won't be. Only 54 percent of accepted college students will finish their degrees even in six years. In 1998, teens predicted that they'd be earning, on average, $75,000 a year by the time they are thirty. But in that year, 2010, the median income of a thirty-year-old was $27,500.

One college grad put it well: "My parents gave me absolutely everything—except the understanding life isn't fair." One great Jewish wisdom saying is, "The best way to get God laughing is to tell him your plans."

When you find a friend—especially a spouse—who trusts your love enough to suggest you just might be over the line, grapple that friend to your soul with hoops of steel. You've found the greatest treasure on earth. And you're just as gifted if that friend is also the self you befriend. Ray Bradbury describes that kind of freeing honesty:

"We're all fools," said Clemens, "all the time. It's just we're a different kind each day. We think, I'm not a fool today. I've learned my lesson. I was a fool yesterday but not this morning. Then tomorrow we find out that, yes, we were a fool today too. I think the only way we can grow and get on in this world is to accept the fact we're not perfect and live accordingly."

That's what people call "the wisdom that comes with age." Surely, if there's no other lesson the years have made less deniable than gravity and death, it's our need to cope with the world we've been given, not the one we dreamed. After all these years, I'm pretty sure the toughest lesson to learn is that someone else is God—someone else made up the rules of the game, introduced a species, which by its very nature *knows* it's imperfect. It takes quite a number of occasions before anyone becomes convinced that—if anyone at all is in charge—it's surely not me.

Winsome pessimist Kurt Vonnegut poses a truth in the *Credo of the Ghost Shirt Society:*

> That there must be virtue in imperfection, because man is imperfect, and man is a creation of God. That there must be virtue in frailty, for man is frail, and man is a creation of God. That there must be virtue in brilliance followed by stupidity, for man is alternately brilliant and stupid, and man is a creation of God.

Because of all that—and Jesus' undeniable preference for Peter the stumbler over the shrewd Judas and the ethereal John, I wonder if it's entirely inappropriate to propose a couple more beatitudes. Like "Blessed—and easily forgiven—are the incautious, who revere the truth so much that they blurt it out. Blessed—and easily forgiven—are those who care so passionately that their hearts have to be put back together again and again. Blessed—and easily forgiven—are those whose fierce commitment makes them intolerable to the proper and prudent." Like the woman known as a sinner who wept on Jesus' feet, "Much is forgiven them because they have loved much." And I pray that the unguarded, the battered but unbroken, the plainspoken and undiplomatic may be allowed legitimate places, even at the end of the line, when the virginal and destitute and demure ease into the Kingdom to which this great bumbler was entrusted the keys.

Have you noticed there's nothing whatever in nature that's a flawless square or circle or diamond? Only human artifacts aspire to that. Every snowflake in Antarctica is exactly the same, but each is completely unique. Even the planets are imperfect spheres. Thank God daily that he made everything imperfect. How dull life would be if every tree in the forest were a perfect cylinder, every apple a sphere, every forester Brad Pitt. A perfect reality would negate the possibility of stories. And the Creator who gave humans freedom must dote on stories.

Apparently, it's not only okay to be imperfect—even to continue being imperfect—but it's impossible to be anything else and remain human. God not only created us that way but freely chose to become imperfect with us. Any crucifix demonstrates that being Christian isn't about achieving; it's about not quitting.

8.

Genuine Humility

*When you have done all that you were ordered
to do, say, "We are worthless slaves; we've done
only what we ought to have done!"*
—Luke 17:10

That little passage flies violently in the face of what the world—
our society—has brainwashed us to accept as the only road to fulfillment: Climb that golden ladder, even if you must crunch the
knuckles of anybody in your way. Domination means survival. Me
first! (Hard to shift from that attitude when you went home from
work each night to the spouse and kids, yes?)

The same Jesus said, "If you want the first place, take the last
place." It begins to sound disconcertingly consistent. Them first:
God and neighbor. We're here subservient to their needs, above
our own.

At the other end of the madness spectrum, the professionally
pious love to run with those gospel segments. "Oh, I'm really nobody. . . . You must understand. I was raised to be reserved. . . . Oh,
I could never." For many years, in the quiet of my soul, despite the
fact I'd vowed myself to God perpetually, I felt a true deficiency
because I am "less a full Christian" than men who drive jeeps in
leper colonies or run soup kitchens in barrios.

So many truly good folks have done the best they could, but
still feel inadequate. "If only I could do better." How can you do
better than your best? Some Hindu women used to practice sut-
tee, hurling themselves on their husband's funeral pyres to prove
the totality of their love and fidelity. (No reports husbands did the
same.) Wanting to give 110 percent is definitively dumb.

I also wasted a great part of my life trying to make excuses for
being "learned and clever," almost as if it were some kind of ge-
netic curse, like being a werewolf. The pious folk who flog the well-
off and educated with the "lilies of the field" quite readily forget if

the Lazarus family had been indigent, Jesus and his friends would have gone hungry. And those who counsel slavish acceptance of insults and exploitation forget that the very same Jesus hounded out the money changers with nothing but a fistful of rope and his own towering rage.

If there's any obstacle to the fulfillment of an already good Christian, *the* surest weapon—hands down—is humility and politeness. When well-intentioned (dumb) people quote Jesus saying, "We're unworthy servants," did they have their fingers in their ears when the very *same* Jesus said he wanted us to climb to the rooftops and *shout* our freedom from the fear of sin and death? They didn't crucify Jesus because he was so meek and mild.

The best way to short-circuit a crusade to set the world's souls on fire is a concerted campaign to get all the candidates to bow their heads and groan, "Oh, I'm nobody!" But that's what kindly folks have whispered to me since I was in diapers: "Don't be proud! Don't get *vain!*" (Even today college students wince with recollection when I quote that.) What could be more un-Christian? Look what the One Calling Us managed to get out of Abraham and Sarah, who were in their nineties and barren as a pair of bricks. And Moses, who stammers for about fifty lines, trying to weasel out of the invitation. And poor dumb Jeremiah trying to beg off because "I'm only a kid!" All heroes were unlikely prospects: Our Lady, St. Peter, Joan of Arc, Francis of Assisi, Martin Luther King, John XXIII, Nelson Mandela, Mother Teresa—all faceless nobodies who finally said, "I'm mad as hell, and I'm not gonna *take* it anymore!" And all those little nobodies upended the world. Jumped up and down and made the parade take a new tack.

"Lord, I'm not worthy you should enter under my roof, *but* only speak the word, and my soul shall be healed." Did you forget that "but"? Your worthiness is no more to the point than the mud and spit Jesus used to cure real blindness. Your sense of unworthiness is, in fact, the biggest obstacle!

Remember, the Latin root of both "humble" and "human" (and "humor") is *humus.* It means *dirt.* Ponder the wondrous, creative, bountiful qualities of earth seething with life. It's not just its ability to provide food but its inner excitement of atoms and muons and gluons sparking around like a gazillion universes in a single clot of humble earth.

Psst! In you, too.

"Humble" and "human" mean "down-to-earth." No pretense, no masks, no defensiveness—as Jesus says, "what is revealed to the merest children": wonder, awe, incautious, able to find "a world in a grain of sand." Saying "I'm nobody" is a monstrous insult to our great-souled Creator. I'm forced to wonder, too, if "humility" might just be a misapplied label for cowardice.

"Oh, I'm too old now." Sez who?

Back in the seminary, when we were only thirty, Larry Madden and I wrote a musical every year as an antidote to madness. One year, with total *hubris*, we did *The Odyssey*, and I wrote a lyric for Odysseus and his old friend, Eumaeus, refusing to give up the challenges of being human:

You just get to feelin' your way around
And your memory starts slippin' away.
You get your two feet down on the ground
And the kids find your feet in the way.
I don't mind the feelin' I'm growin' old.
It's hard, after all, bein' young.
But I don't like feelin' left out in the cold
With so many flings unflung.
They say it's too late in the year for flings.
I haven't too many more springs.
Well maybe the sun is about to set
There's plenty of fun in the old boys yet.

Any virtue, unbalanced by its opposite, becomes a vice. Justice without mercy degrades into vengeance; mercy unalloyed with justice becomes sentimentality; celibacy without passion becomes sterility. Reductionism is always easier to practice—and teach— than the complex truth. Marxism is an admirable ideal, except that it leaves out original sin. Monopoly capitalism really works, as long as you ignore human dignity.

Humility unchecked by honest self-esteem becomes joyless servitude, robotic perseverance, factoring one's own self-worth *out* of any judgment. Unadulterated pride resolutely refuses to admit its real faults; unadulterated humility just as resolutely refuses to admit its real virtues. There's a third state of soul, usually in the good-hearted trying their very best to serve God, a perverse amalgam of the two: a dread of vanity so deep-seated that it becomes (usually without the victim's awareness) prideful self-abasement. "Just give them a mirror."

Most of us trying to serve the Kingdom, like St. Paul, have enough "thorns in our sides" we needn't fear *hubris*. And most of us nearing the crest have had far more practice at fault-finding even than we had back in totally self-obsessed adolescence.

Yet those with a penchant for finding motes in others' eyes are quick to label anyone confident in service as "prideful, arrogant, vain," and too often those possessed of such confidence are themselves tormented by the possibility their critics might be right. In a similar way, those who take seriously Ignatius Loyola's admonition to labor "for the *greater* glory of God" are subject to accusations of being perennial gripers about changing "the way things are."

I'd suggest that pride isn't the root of all evil. Lack of it is. Who with any honest sense of self-respect and esteem would ever degrade that sacred self by cheating, snorting dope, clicking on Internet porn? I have a hunch that if those kind people who formed us had made us honestly proud rather than fearful of divine rejection, we'd have lived in—and handed on—a happier world.

Consider the paradox in scripture itself. On the one hand, "The servant does not deserve thanks," and on the other, "Let your light shine!" In our upbringing, the former got far more attention than the latter. It's not too late to change that.

St. Paul, I think, balances the paradox: "In union with Christ Jesus, then, I can be *proud* of my service to God" (Romans 15:17). Xavier Leon-Dufour defines pride as "a noble attitude which originates in an awareness of election, manifested in an upright bearing, a head held high, and, especially, in clear speech and confident behavior." Christian assurance comes from the call of our baptism and from our personal confirmation of its mission. That call infuses confidence in my own lifelong experience, my skills, my unique ability to serve the enrichment of the Kingdom. It's the confidence that leads to self-forgetfulness, that led Peter to step onto the water when Jesus invited him to. It's captured in the exuberance of *The Magnificat.*

But that confidence, that energizing pride in one's service, can't come from the outside, from the thanks of others, awards, degrees, publications, not even from God himself. Unless I'm humble enough to *accept* God's confidence in me, like accepting God's forgiveness, it can never become effective, life-giving, igniting joy. I've tied God's hands. And my own.

We forget that, throughout the scriptures, God chose his messengers despite—or perhaps even *because of*—their shortcomings, as he did with Adam and Eve, Noah, Abram and Sarai, Moses, Gideon, David, and as Jesus chose Peter, Judas, Thomas, and James and John, the "sons of thunder," with the other seven who also hiked up their skirts and ran from him.

It's difficult for the lifetime Catholic to accept that truth, because of years of well-intentioned catechesis and their own lack of time and provocation to critique it as adults. Pride in our lives is justified by the humility to accept that the One who has chosen us believes us worthy of the call that ennobles those lives.

It's crucial to remember: Even though none of us is essential, each of us is important.

And our best has to be good enough. It's all we have.

9.

Incarnational Reality

*Nicodemus said to him, "How can anyone
be born after having grown old? Can one enter
a second time into the mother's womb and be
born?"*

—John 3:4

If we can sidestep literalism, the answer to Nicodemus is a reso-
nant, "Yes!" Not only can you go back, but according to Jesus, it's
essential. Unless you do, you can't even access the remote suburbs
of his "Kingdom." By "the Kingdom," he meant not just faraway
heaven, as we were instructed so long ago, but our *purpose* here
and now, the reason we were born. By "eternal life," Jesus meant
"what it's all about," success, fulfillment, happiness, Reality as
God understands that.

What will make humans wag their tails with joy like retrievers,
even when they're exhausted—because they're doing what they
were born to do?

Jesus told Nicodemus that we—who have for a lifetime iden-
tified success-fulfillment-happiness-Really-Real with Progress! . . .
More! . . . Higher!—have to retool our convictions about those values. Accepting Christ is accepting—brace yourself!—that you win
by losing. "If you want the first place, take the last place." The world
beater must go back for basic lessons from a child: awe, wonder, vulnerability. The definitive hero of Christianity conquers, paradoxically, by surrendering. So to deal as a Christian with God, we sophis-
ticated, painfully (and expensively) educated adults have to go back
and relearn lessons (attitudes, really) we learned before kindergarten and forgot. Or more likely thought we outgrew them or found
such attitudes blissfully naive in a dog-eat-dog reality—which we
gradually, unconsciously accepted as if that were The Really Real.

All I Ever Needed to Know I Learned in Kindergarten (Fulghum,
1986). Being a decent human being—fully alive—requires very

simple convictions. And convictions are only peripherally affected by the insights one finds in even the best tutorial books. Some Christian insights open up only on field trips: hangin' out with Jesus himself. Hacking away all the undergrowth and sucker vines laid on over the basic message by well-meaning catechisms, religious education, homilies, diocesan newspapers, that have smothered the message of the God-man about how to be human. Being *super*human, Christlike, has even fewer precepts than we were taught. That just comes down to the self-confidence to put others ahead of yourself. Supernatural means extrahuman.

What does a child have just by *nature*, before the commercials get in there and screw up their wired-in gyroscopes? For one thing, attentiveness. Just watch a baby's eyes flicker around at all the miracles. Astonishment. Until they get jaded—until they start taking things for granted, like being spoiled—most of their lives are breathtaking, like that first slap-induced gasp at birth that made them breathe and live. And then, just by nature, with no need to induce it, they exult in making sounds and falling in love with them. Then, like Helen Keller, comes the explosive insight that words carry *meaning*, that words throw out grappling hooks to other hearts and minds, that they make you less afraid of the as yet unknown. (Until we start shackling them to grades.)

How much do older people have to *unlearn*? I once heard a flight attendant make an announcement worthy of the Sybil of Delphi: "This is the most difficult moment of your week. Please turn off all electronic devices." Imagine the global insanity if some satanic terrorist discovered a way to neutralize every battery on earth. The world of cutthroat capitalism would short-circuit and plummet into the abyss. Suddenly, the real stars would jump out of the sky from the neon haze over our cities. Millions of teenagers would run amok, crazed by the silence.

Christianity goes a warp-speed distance beyond morality, justice, humanity. Those of us long embroiled in the jungle of cities must stretch beyond even the incalculably enormous physical universe(s) to the beyond, the transcendent Realm from which Jesus came to remind us of that Dimension and invite us into it forever. Been there lately? It's been there all along.

We've all been spattered with "religion," recently only in sermons but years ago in a swamp of cutesy Bible lessons and turgid catechisms, concepts totally foreign to "real life." Such ideas as *soul, holiness, sacred, supernatural* were as common and unexplained as sex and gravity.

I can't personally recall anyone explaining even in any vague way what those "unreal" concepts meant. But everyone who appealed to them made it painfully clear they were very, very crucial indeed. Even in four suffocating years of graduate theology courses, I never remember a single professor speaking of God as a personal Friend, only as a rarefied Entity. I can't recall a single one who spoke of praying, except if tapped for an annual retreat. The classroom and chapel were as distant from one another as Alpha Centauri and Buford, WY.

But this book is an attempt to tap into a "supernatural *life*," becoming friends with a God whom we've all faithfully served quite some time now. For many of us now beyond our formal education, God and all those impractical spiritual realities were "out there," like Boolean geometry and voodoo. And even for those of us who have formidable degrees and decades of hard-won expertise in other fields still believe "supernatural" means something "above" like "superstructure" or "way up in heaven." Rather it means our nature "superenergized." The white-hot innermost core of Christianity holds that the Son of God crossed that abyss between other-worldly and this-worldly. He *fused* them. Just as, from the primal explosion, the universe has been "charged with the grandeur of God," now so is humanity. "In him all things hold together" (Colossians 1:17). The Creator of Alpha Centauri now has many residences in Buford, WY.

Human nature, all by itself, is an invitation (not a command as with all other natures) to act better than other animals, or vegetables, or stones. And since the only nature we have is human nature, "supernatural" has to mean an invitation beyond just being decent, moral, empathic, kind *humans*—to being human in a hyperenergized way. More *intensely* decent, moral, empathic, kind. In fact it means—in a superclumsy metaphor—living with one foot firmly planted in the day-to-day real and the other planted in The

Really Real that God inhabited before space and time and feet had any meaning. Not totally unlike the single citizen of Buford inviting an Alpha Centaurian to supper. (Actually, even more unimaginable than that!) Recall the verse on the epigraph page: "I don't call you servants any longer. You are my friends" (John 15:15). Think of so many gospel invitations to a banquet. The Last Supper and every Eucharist is an invitation from the Master to the field hands to come inside and sit right down with the Trinity family and the whole communion of saints. His invitation *makes* you worthy.

Christianity is a different quality of living, a different vigor, a radically different *orientation*. Like the bishop in *Les Miserables*, who not only forgave Jean Valjean for stealing his silverware, but gave him the silverware, plus two silver candlesticks he'd neglected to steal. Jesus never once asked a sinner to grovel, or to give an exhaustive list of sins, or asked a sinner for a retributive penance. That's light years beyond justice.

We need time to get *back* down to more basic stuff—like withdrawal from the everyday hurly-burly that's seemed the limit of reality most of our lives and to do some basic reindoctrination toward The Really Real. Jesus said, "Truly I tell you, unless you change and become like children, you will never enter the kingdom of heaven" (Matthew 18:3).

Most children have a much, much vaster dimension to life ingrained in their nature from the first instant their eyes pop open in amazement. And good parents feed that soul hunger with all kinds of color and flash and sounds. The life of enchantment. And those burgeoning souls bristle with creativity, conjuring universes out of empty cardboard boxes. And if all goes well, that exciting sense of curiosity goes hungrily on—gobbling up life and transforming it as God did with nothing at the beginning. The child keeps growing more intensely human. For a while.

That lasts till second grade. Maybe age six? After that, it's all downhill. Every vacant face you see on a subway car was once energized by that magic. So sad. No wonder zombie films have become so popular. It's the same fellow feeling evoked in Kafka's *Metamorphosis*.

About second grade, graduates of teachers' colleges take over. Then life becomes a serious business. Some utterly befuddled parents yank their privileged children from Wonderland and enroll them in courses to beef up their left brains with word lists and fractions in service of the draconian SATs. Quickly, Muppets and Disney folks give way to the Empiricists and Thomas Gradgrind. Calculus on one side and *Jersey Shore* on the other, with little between. Now, information preempts—often precludes—understanding. Even Freudians betrayed their master and made sure everywhere he wrote "soul" they translated as a more acceptable "mind." Difficult today to label anything generally accepted as "sacred." The Super Bowl maybe.

The clues in this book are meant to be a treasure map to rediscover your own soul.

For some, long restrained by caring for others from the luxury of time to pause and ponder—to reestablish their citizenship in the Fifth Dimension—that means a screeching halt. Then shifting to reverse, tooling back and reminding oneself I even *have* a soul—or more rightly *am* a soul. The soul is who I am—my innermost, truest *me*. My "self" is the most important monument to my having lived, the essence of me I trust can walk through the doorway of death.

My soul is what the educational process—at its profoundest—*should* have been evolving. But we all know that, too often, that process yielded to the efficiency of job certification, learning how to make a living, sidestepping learning what living is *for*. A tragic loss, but not due to anyone's malice. Merely a surrender to more urgent, practical issues. If that happened to you, this book may help set that right. Or make it a little less shallow and askew.

Once you grasp your essence—that heaven-hungry soul—then you can take the time to dally with questions missing for most of your religious training—all those "values" we've always claimed were essential to full humanity but quite likely never once pondered: gratitude, empathy, kindness, endurance, and many more essential-but-unfocused aspects of growing into what God created humans to be. Life is now an *elderhostel* for enrichment.

The body gurgles for food, the mind itches for answers, and

the spirit expresses its hunger in restlessness and discontent. So, if you're suffering from the blahs or nothing makes any sense anymore or one damn thing after another, you likely suffer from soul malnutrition. The hungers of the body can be temporarily assuaged by cheese puffs and soft drink, the hungers of the mind by ball-scores and gossip, and the hungers of the soul by soap operas and soft-core porn. But the result of bad food and lack of exercise are the same for all three: flab. What you need is to exercise the one thing that separates us from beasts: the soul—reaching out into the Beyond.

10.
Humor: Accepting the Absurd

Common sense and a sense of humor are the
same thing, moving at different speeds. A sense
of humor is just common sense, dancing.
—William James

Any virtue—unbalanced by its opposite—runs amok into a vice. Just so, dignity needs the corrective of humor—*humus.* That fusion of dignity and humility was intended to separate Adam and Eve from their shrewdest fellow creatures: perspective. (The original sin was losing that perspective on what's what.)

It was all there in the Genesis story, the part our kindly religious teachers bypassed in order to get to the fascinating, paralyzing *sin* stuff. They were keen on emphasizing that we were made out of mud (Genesis 2:7), a grim perspective buffered every Ash Wednesday with "Dust thou art and into dust thou shalt return." They probably hadn't had enough modern cosmology to know it was *star*dust. But what they avoided was the second half of the *same* verse! "He breathed into his nostrils the breath of life." We're not only made of stardust, but we have the breath (Heb: *ruah*, Gk: *psyche*, Lat: *anima*) of God in us, too! God's Spirit. *In us!*

That insight flies directly in the face of the punitive, vindictive God of John Calvin, who finds all but God's arbitrarily chosen elect/pets detestable. It rejects Luther who said that, even after Christ, we're still dung, our filth hidden from God by Christ's merits like a layer of snow. And it rejects the Irish crypto-Calvinist Jansenists who trained those who trained us. And it shunned an understanding of the so-perfect deist God of Plato and Eastern mystics whose God is so utterly "other" one can't legitimately even use the word "is" about both God and humans.

No. Even before the advent of the Son of God, humans were

made of stardust and Godlife! And then (because for about thirty thousand years we kept underselling our value), God immersed himself into humanity with all its filth, corruption, confusion, agony, even death, trying his divine best to give us the widest perspective within which to judge our value.

Few of us past midlife were ever pushed to balance our faults with our being loved unconditionally. Balance, perspective, impartiality.

The Greeks found the same bedrock: *meden agan*—"nothing in excess." No matter how far God's evolution invites us into rationality, we always drag the wondrous, erratic, goofy, creative, insatiable, embarrassing, impulsive, reason-defiant flesh along. The same flesh the Son of God freely chose to enter and share with us.

Without a sense of the ludicrous, the human condition is unbearable, as reading any gifted atheist proves. Without a God who loves not only logic but the absurd, they're left to believe that logic itself leads only to despair. As Albert Camus insisted, in a godless universe, the two greatest curses are intelligence and hope—because there are no true answers and no one survives. Thus, he says, the only true philosophical question is finding a reason not to commit suicide.

His despair would have been so easily healed had he the courage and humility to yield center stage to someone else. If I'm *not* Nietzsche's *Ubermensch*, if some Other has that burden and gives purpose to each of the game pieces—even me—then I not only have to (honestly) accept the bitter with the sweet but the comedic with the tragic. That might be one of *the* greatest hurdles of adolescence: getting beyond posturing in lonely misunderstood-hood and learning the grace to laugh at oneself. Not the bitter chuckles one gets from the wit of *Waiting for Godot*, but the belly laughs from saints of sanity like the Marx Brothers, Victor Borge, and Carol Burnett.

If you allow for a God, he/she/they surely *must* enjoy a joke. Anybody who could invent the hairy-nosed wombat, the giraffe, *and* sex had to have done so giggling. And let's not embarrass the poor platypus. Or penguins. "Glory be to me! Wait till they get hold of *this* one!" And the evidence in the universe for a reasoning-but-untrappably playful God is escapable only by reductionism, denying significant evidence. Everywhere in the universe, every object is engaged in the same *patterned dance*—turning on its own axis, in a pas-de-deux with a moon or two, circling another set, all in a near-infinite, *predictable* carouse. Yet no two participants are alike: some glacial, others fiery, some mere dust, at least one glowing watery blue. Order and *surprise*. "Catch me if you can!" Everyone has fingerprints and DNA, but each set is unique. Every snowflake in Antarctica (Count 'em!) is the same pattern, except no two are exactly the same. No two people see precisely the same film or read the same book.

Aren't we lucky God is not the chill watchmaker of the deists? Boring!

One corrective to humorless self-centeredness is yielding to the truth that, although you're usually unaware of it, you're traveling eastward right this minute at 750 miles an hour (more or less, depending on how far you are from the equator). And it doesn't mess up your hair. If you shrunk the history of the cosmos to a single year beginning with the Big Bang at 12:00:01 on January 1, your sixty years start on December 31 at about 11:59:59:50. Pfft!

Against that background, our pretensions to tragedy are horribly out of proportion. Neil Armstrong, the first moonwalker, wrote of looking from there to earth: "It suddenly struck me that that tiny pea, pretty and blue, was the Earth. I put up my thumb and shut one eye, and my thumb blotted out the planet Earth. I didn't feel like a giant. I felt very, very small." And yet the mythologist Joseph Campbell gives a corrective to that: "With our view of earthrise, we could see that the earth and the heavens were no longer divided but that the earth is in the heavens." And if we add to that what we claim has been our belief all along, beyond it all is a loving Creator who knows each of our names, then every tragedy ends up a comedy.

Most atheists I've read are brilliant thinkers, inspired stylists, but so damned humorless, stodgy. (And the "damned" is justified.) I've often wondered how they deal with children—who defy reason and yield only to the common sense most mothers seem to have, inbred. I also wonder how atheists explain stand-by-me unselfish love—which out and out defies reason.

Oedipus was apparently the sharpest guy in Thebes—calculus smart, razor-sharp smart, riddle-smart, *Jeopardy*-smart. I read Sophocles' play about him twice—line by line, in Greek—once in college, then (agonizingly) in the seminary. I hated him—and the play. (It wasn't *just* the Greek!) Oedipus was such a smug know-it-all. (I roomed with a guy just like that.) No genuine *feelings*. Oh, lots of moans and groans for his poor plague-ridden subjects. To me, most of it felt faked—it was so operatic. And the poseur claimed *his* agony about *their* agony was even more unbearable. Like Christopher Hitchens and Richard Dawkins, he was so mesmerized by his own (genuine) brilliance, he thought he could set a limit to what he'd allow to be real. He'd outwitted the gods (he was certain); therefore, "This town ain't big enough for both of us."

I taught the play to Advanced Placement English seniors for about twenty years, then I got a jolt of common sense and pulled myself up short. I realized I was doing that play only because it reeked of "classicism, in-crowd erudition, snooty." Colleges expected it. Parents could brag that their sons were bright (and polite) enough to endure it in the name of one-upmanship. I finally admitted to a kind of common sense attitude that dared defy what "everybody says," the same as my persnickety blue-collar response to opera, wherein the voices of what seemed real people soar and their gestures befit the savaged and ravished—over a lost key or swabbing the deck. And in one, a tubercular dying seamstress sings with the gusto of a longshoreman as she coughs gouts of her last life's blood. Death to perspective and common sense! I end up giggling.

I finally got fed up with Hamlet's impenetrable narcissism, too. In Holden Caulfield, okay. He was only seventeen. But the script implies in Act V that Hamlet was in his thirties. I finally got some perspective myself and said, "When are you gonna *grow up*, you jerk?" and bade farewell to the gloomy Dane. I turned instead to King Lear, who finally discovered who he really was, under the crown and brocade—at last broke *through* the Oedipus/Hamlet self-enclosure—when he stood raving in the storm, finally being the fool instead of merely playing at it.

I can see why true, eyes-wide-open atheists are so courageously grim and why well-fed, subsidized college atheists can't possibly be anything but imposters. Atheist despair is at least more dignified (and coldly logical) than Oedipus's furious denials and Hamlet's tedious melancholia. If death annihilates everything, if everything you've ever striven for is just so much potential garbage—including you—it tends to dampen the spirit between now and the great simplification. Honest atheists keep turning over every single philosophical rock, convinced there's a nest of serpents underneath. If they find a clutch of sun-hungry crocuses, they grump, "Oh, well. They'll all die soon enough." God knows how suicidal the lugubrious Irish would be without the Blessed Mother. And music. (And whisky.)

Humor comes from a sense of intellectual *perspective*: an awareness that some things are objectively important, others not; and that those two incompatibles are most oddly jumbled in everyday affairs. But—we assume—their mutual abrasion is the will of a purposeful God. Rubbing them together should ignite the Holy Spirit in us.

If you can amble away from the *tyranny* of logic, every glass is completely full, even if half is filled only with air. Or as George Carlin put it, "twice as large as it needs to be." The problems arise when we become full of ourselves.

Until we break through to perspective, back ourselves up out of the spotlight and into supporting roles or even the chorus, we remain as tetchy as *The Princess and the Pea*, unable to relax into a world where there are more joys than there are intrusions on our comfort. As Eliot says, "I am not Prince Hamlet." I used to think I was. Then I thought I might qualify for windy Polonius. But—if I see "things as they truly are"—how lucky I am indeed just to be in the play when I need never have existed at all! Even if I have to take the first curtain calls, play Rosencrantz—and double as Vortigern, Marcellus, and Reynaldo.

It's a cliché that those in bruising professions like police and firefighters and medical examiners, where tragedy rules, have a rough sense of humor about the horrible elements of their professions. Outsiders find it insensitive—when it's precisely their sensitivity that compels it. Some daring psychiatrists tell patients who suffer fierce anxiety attacks to set aside ten minutes a day to feel completely, unguardedly savaged by anxiety: grind their teeth, growl, asphyxiate themselves in terror. When they do sit there, grunting to become wretched, they most often feel simply silly. And laugh. Those who directed attempts at brainwashing in the Soviet Gulag said, "As soon as the subject laughs, the whole process is wrecked and has to begin over again."

Dualism/Reductionism

We would rather be ruined than changed.
We would rather die in our dread than climb
the cross of the present and let our illusions die.
—W. H. Auden

It's called "paradoxical therapy," and nothing could be a more fitting template for truth than paradox. On the contrary, an intolerance for paradox, irony, and ambiguity results in devastating *dualism*—the chill, "witless" division of everything into pairs of iron-walled bins that delight the left brain and repel the right. That half-witted mind governed the church I grew up in, where we were conditioned to believe every misdeed was *either* mortal *or* venial, that is, utterly destructive of one's connection to God or inconsiderably trivial. Thus, according to such minds, a single act of sex with artificial birth control between parents of five children is, ipso facto, equivalent to dynamiting an orphanage. (See? Common sense? Perspective? Giggle.)

They believe that, by defining something or tucking it into a formula (preferably Latinate) they actually understand what the reality *is*, that they then exercise some sort of real *control* over it. Which is as silly as explaining that objects fall because of "gravity" and birds migrate because of "instinct" as if we really understood what the hell we're claiming. Exactly the same could apply to "love," "loyalty," "sin," "grace," "faith," even "God." Labels pasted on wind.

I'll bet money the last time you pondered those realities or had them explained you were still being supported by your parents. Test it out. Try to explain any one of them to a teenager. The univocal, pinched mind simply can't see the difference, for instance, between sex and gender. Most of us use the words interchangeably, as if they were like "dusk" and "evening." Sex is, objectively, in fact, either/or: *physical*. Lift the diaper, there's your unarguable answer. It's a clarity that delights logicians. Gender, though (as anyone who's studied languages—especially those who studied Latin [wink!]—ought to know), is masculine/feminine—not either/or but more/less. Gender is *psychological*, perhaps in some way influenced by physical nature but much more influenced by scrambled nurture. Robert Browning and Hemingway were both virile males, but Browning's sensitivity was more gentle, vulnerable, inclusive, nonjudgmental than Hemingway's. Margaret Thatcher and Princess Diana were both females and mothers, but Thatcher was psychologically more "masculine" than the sad princess.

At least till our most recent pope, my experience of "mother church" has been almost exclusively "masculine," even though it was run exclusively by men in dresses. See? Humorous?

For dualists and literalists, there's no twilight, only night or day, no "sort-of crazy but . . . ," no "guilty, and yet . . . ," no "*pretty* successful," no "not bad at all!" They simply don't get jokes. E. B. White said that analyzing humor is like dissecting a frog. The dissector is little the wiser, and the frog dies. Psychologist Harvey Mindess writes, "Though we make fun of ourselves for being stupid or lazy or klutzy, by laughing at those flaws, what we are really saying is that we're lovable nonetheless."

Richard Rohr, a veritable pursuivant of poisonous reductionism, writes that dualistic thinking is the "well-practiced pattern of knowing most things by comparison. And for some reason, once you compare or label things (that is, judge) you almost always conclude that one is good and the other is less good or even bad." With evident common sense and good humor (and pristine rationality), he offers seven Cs of delusion, suggesting that "the dualistic mind compares, competes, conflicts, conspires, condemns, cancels out any contrary evidence, and crucifies with impunity." Familiar?

That inflexible dualism permeated and blissfully simplified my early Catholic life. Not just male/female (which St. Paul supposedly demolished twenty centuries ago), but black/white, priestly/lay, Jew/Gentile, good/evil, Catholic/damned. "Don't mess with Mister In-Between." This mind-set is binary, like mechanistic computers, which are reliably logical but oughtn't to decide whether to start a war—or such politicians as George W. Bush, who said "I don't 'do' nuance."

In genuine paradoxes, the opposites are not antagonisms but *creative tensions*—for those experienced enough and confident enough to continue to explore and grow. Time at last we outgrow the shackles of the too-easy answers we learned in childhood and never had time or provocation to challenge. For instance, that the disgraceful crucifixion was not a matter of obsequious reparation but a moment of fulfillment and a quantum leap in evolution.

Sometimes they become unwittingly—pun intended—laughable. Flesh vs. Spirit (blame Paul and Augustine there—and Plato—in diametric contradiction to the doctrine of incarnation), God's will vs. change (despite creation, evolution, the shift from Judaism to Christianity), saint vs. sinner (despite the fact Peter was apostate, then pope), orthodox vs. heretic (although Jesus himself and every early disciple was a renegade from Judaism). "Repent" ipso facto demands "rethink" all your certitudes, even the ones the official church forbids to be rethought. Orthodoxy without flexibility and doubt becomes fascism. Funny-strange, not funny-ha-ha. But those are the conundrums that keep systematic theologians in food, clothing, and shelter.

When—precisely—does "East" become "West"? "Venial" become "mortal"? "With us" become "against us"? Is an electron a wave or a particle? Are humans angels or beasts? Could Hitler squeeze into heaven? Giggle. Wanna bet he's there now, playing with Jewish kids?

Is it possible you personally have superimposed your childhood God on the Real Thing?

The Tao: Fusing Contradictions

You likely have heard of the *Tao*, the Confucian belief that means "The Way." I'm sure you've seen its symbol: a circle divided by a wavy line, one half white, one half black—but each with a small circle of the other color: a balance within each individual of the aggressive, decisive, rational, so-called masculine by psychologists like Carl Jung, and the embracing, intuitive, creative, so-called feminine. It's a basis for all human activity, for morality, for establishing a sense of personal worth. In the ideal, it's a perfect, fluid harmony within each human, among humans, and within nature, everyone and everything doing what their inner constitution reveals that they're intended to: in balance. The world as it ought to be: a synthesis of rest and movement. Its flexible complementarity is the diametric opposite of pernicious Western dualism. The *Yang* is hot, clear and dry, rambunctious, male, and the *Yin* is cool, moist, receptive, dark, rest, water, earth, female. A total balance.

However, the great Plato wrote that "if anyone represents men of worth as overpowered by laughter we must *not* accept it, much less of gods." And the Rule of St. Benedict, the most influential of monastic codes, calls for strict control of laughter. One monastery demanded these punishments: "He who smiles in the service . . . six strokes; if he breaks out in the noise of laughter, a special fast unless it has happened pardonably." In Hebrew scripture, God laughs only in scorn, as in Psalm 37:13, "But the Lord laughs at the wicked, for he sees their day is coming." Despite the unseemly delight in someone's impending doom (Google: *Schadenfreude*), that divine attitude is consistent with my own early-life image of a God of ink-stained fingers with a great ledger at the top of my tightrope, sniggering at my clumsiness, just waiting.

Closer to our own time, listen to that true humanist-humorist, the Ayatollah Khomeini:

Allah did not create man so he could have fun. The aim
of creation was for mankind to be put to the test through
hardship and prayer. An Islamic regime must be serious
in every field. There are no jokes in Islam. There is no
humor in Islam. There is no fun in Islam. There can be
no fun and joy in whatever is serious.

Tell me you didn't give at least an internal snort reading that.
Think of the cramped, arid lives of the sadistic inquisitors, the
Salem witch burners, the casual Holocaust murderers.

And for a lifetime, we've at least professed that Jesus is the
Way to eternal life, human fulfillment, and there are those mirth-
less Pecksniffs who insist Jesus never laughed. True, even the most
meticulous survey of the Old Testament reveals a God who laughs
only in scorn, but I find that accusation laid on Jesus edging dan-
gerously into heresy. Probably the most critical Christian belief is
that Jesus the Nazareth carpenter was truly divine *and* truly man.
But any human who never laughs, who sees only the tragic side,
has very serious psychological problems, doesn't deserve credence
from real humans.

Nonetheless, the somber Jesus was the only one whose image the official church would allow to be bought and sold, for the
same reason the Nazis never showed Hitler smiling. We're training obedient boys and girls here, who don't act up or ask difficult
questions. We will subsidize no images of Jesus whipping out the
souvenir sellers, surely no spittle spattering from his mouth as he
curses out the clergy. There will be no animal droppings in Christmas scenes.

Such one-sidedness is not only ludicrous but utterly repellent
to anyone to whom God gave wits. Just as Jesus had to eat and
grow fatigued, he *had* to laugh. Simply to qualify as fully human,
Jesus had to be tempted, had to doubt, had to suffer; he also had
to snicker at the silliness "all flesh is heir to." The humorless quote
the Beatitudes (of course out of context): "Woe to you who are
laughing now, for you will mourn and weep" (Luke 6:26), as if
Jesus were a Methodist—in defiance of the evidence that his enemies called him a glutton and a drunkard. They fail to see he
wasn't condemning laughter any more than he was praising weep-

ing. (The same folks make a similar slip when they quote him about poverty and wealth.) And they completely ignore the previous verse that offers laughter as a reward for those who now weep. Context. Perspective.

He performed his first miracle to provide alcohol to keep a party going. Though he was by definition sinless, he had a shocking lack of criticism and an excess of empathy with weakness, especially sexual weakness. His good-natured patience with his thick-headed apprentices is astonishing, and calling a vaunting teddy bear like Simon Peter "Rocky" was far from literal. Could anybody have looked up into that sycamore tree at Zaccheus's piggy Danny DeVito astonishment and not giggle? Jesus was dabbling in the same kind of comedy as Laurel and Hardy when he pictured a fat millionaire trying to herniate himself through the eye of a needle, and Norman Rockwell could have painted a snotty prig with a magnifying glass poking for a speck of dust in his neighbor's eye, ignoring the log poking from his own eye. Jesus had the same delight in deflating the Pharisees as Shakespeare had with Malvolio and the Marx Brothers had with long-suffering, completely out-of-it Margaret Dumont.

That's *funny*, gang! At least to folks not blinded by their own position and erudition.

You can't feel anxious, angry, or sad when you're laughing, allowing you to see situations in a more realistic, less threatening light. A humorous perspective creates psychological distance, which can help you avoid feeling overwhelmed.

Smile. Fake it till you feel it. Share your embarrassing moments. The best way to take yourself less seriously is to talk about times when you took yourself too seriously. While you might think taking the weight of the world on your shoulders is admirable, in the long run it's unrealistic, unproductive, unhealthy, and even egotistical.

Thomas More once said, "The devil, the evil spirit, cannot endure to be mocked." There is no better way to turn away the darkness than by using humor. If you refuse to take them seriously, they'll find it difficult to find an inroad into your consciousness.

Camus, who couldn't seem to grasp the anguish of nihilism

firmly enough to be fully atheist, wrote, "When you have once seen the glow of happiness on the face of a beloved person, you know that a man can have no vocation but to awaken that light on the faces surrounding him. In the depth of winter, I finally learned that within me there lay an invincible summer."

11.
Praying as an Adult

Prayer is not asking. It is a longing of soul,
daily admission of one's weakness. It is better
in prayer to have heart without words than
words without heart.

—Mahatma Gandhi

The only time praying has seemed needful for most of us adults is when we're in need of a handout or answers. "But God doesn't give me what I ask or solve my problems." Forgetting, of course, that "No" really is an answer and that God's silence might be saying, "Look. What did I give *you* a brain for?"

I've pretty much given up prayers of petition, since I said Mass every day for three years that my mother could die, and she didn't. Nothing wrong with petitions. The Best of Us prayed in Gethsemane for release from the torment ahead. The difference was Jesus knew God wasn't going to yield to his prayers. Like Mary at Cana, simply telling a friend there was a need.

Childish Expectations

When you share sorrow with bereaved friends, they don't expect you to bring back the dead. They draw strength from you to go on, because you let them know they're not alone. God doesn't play the game for us, just lets us know—if we allow it—we're not alone and helps us realize the game's played in a larger context than we're usually aware of. Sometimes we prattle along so much, God must say, "Look, I'll try to suggest a few things if you'll only shut up and *listen!*"

Some things in your life you can never change—your DNA, family, past mistakes. Until you face the truth of that, you can never be free to grow. But some things can be changed—bad habits, procrastination, poor self-image. When you think something's unchangeable, then you need a friend you can tell, "I've run out of wine. I've run out of courage . . . hope . . . love."

It means admitting, when you most hate to, that—at least now—you can't do it alone. The only alternative is slogging on, day after day, stewing in your own wretchedness, hurling petitions across the endless cold of space to an inaccessible heaven, where the lines are always busy.

One source of help is being humble enough to reach out to one of us. It's what we're here for. We're here to love you, until you're capable again of loving yourself. And there's always Christ at your elbow.

Like turning water into wine, turning fear into confidence, or discouragement into hope, or self-distaste into self-forgetfulness may seem utterly impossible. It's not. The profoundest gift from prayer is the conviction you're never—ever—alone. Ask Christ to stiffen your weakness.

However, there is a time-honored caveat that applies especially when one prays to God as an adult rather than as a child: "Be careful what you pray for." And an anonymous verse shows how inventive God can be:

I asked for strength
and God gave me difficulties to make me strong.
I asked for wisdom,
and God gave me problems to solve.
I asked for prosperity,
and God gave me a brain and the energy to work.
I asked for courage,
and God gave me dangers to overcome.
I asked for love,
and God gave me troubled people to help.
I received nothing I wanted,
but I received everything I needed.

Think of the time in your life when—to your mutual surprise—you and your parents were no longer treating one another as provider and dependent, but rather as adult to adult. Never quite equals, but no longer relating *around* differences, but instead easygoing as friends who've shared a very great deal. If God's providence was heading us toward adulthood, one can imagine he also hoped to deal with us sooner or later friend to friend.

Incarnation: Still Awesome, but Accessible

In the process, you can be forming a felt friendship with the "subject" of theology, belief, and organized religion. Without that friendship, religious education was as cold and gray and lifeless as geometry or statistics, and—for too many—worship becomes a dutiful party for a guest of honor who never seems to show up. Not *really*.

Therefore, adult praying should be an attempt to establish that *transcosmic* connection.

But I, for one, have difficulty dealing *personally* with the everywhere God. And didn't. But Jesus made that "distance" no longer as daunting. He *became* flesh. To put it perhaps too concretely, the unspeakable majesty of creation humbled himself and depended on the loving-kindness of others to change his diapers. With the only exception of willful departure from God—sin—God can now say, wholeheartedly, "Right! Me, too!" Like all your lifetime friends. And "Hi! I'm here. Let's go for a walk."

This divine accessibility isn't really as novel as it might seem to those of us both educated and Catholic, but not "educated Catholics." From all reports, it began quite some time ago, long before the incarnation. Reports suggest Yahweh enjoyed a stroll with Adam and Eve around their idyllic property in the cool of the evening (Genesis 3:8). He stopped around to the tent of Abram and Sarai infuriatingly often with vague promises of impossible fruition in their sterile old age. What's more, in the question of blasting Sodom and Gomorrah, Yahweh submitted for what must have taken hours to that same patriarch "jewing him down" about it. Yahweh wrestled with Jacob all night long, like a pair of touch-hungry teenage boys (Genesis 22:34), heedless of his own celestial dignity. And that genial bickering between the Creator and his persnickety creatures continued for millennia, through such unqualified disputants as Moses, Gideon, Jonah, even Job, Isaiah, Jeremiah (for thirty chapters!)—all of whom, politely, suggested to their great friend that he was making a huge mistake in his choice of pals and emissaries. In *The Sparrow*, Mary Doria Russell pictures an ancient understanding of God I found only later in life:

> The Jewish sages also tell us that God dances when His children defeat Him in argument, when they stand on their feet and use their minds. . . . To ask them is a very fine kind of human behavior. If we keep demanding that God yield up His answers, perhaps some day we will understand them. And then we will be something more than clever apes, and we shall dance with God.

For three years his apostles and disciples spent days and especially uneventful nights with the incarnate Christ, in ways the gospels found too peripheral to their main purpose to record: bathing together (quite close to naked), sleeping by campfires bunched together against the cold, sharing bread day after day, huddling in caves from a storm, enduring the repulsive types Jesus not only attracted but sought out, putting up with the thoughtless importunities of people whose problems were the only problems on earth.

Ignatius Loyola suggests a method of prayer to obliterate further the distance between the Everywhere God and the Word Made Flesh. It uses the *imagination*—a precious human faculty infrequently accessed by theology professors and catechists—to lessen the gap between our souls and the incandescent-but-incarnate Spirit of Christ. He calls it "composition of place," trying to focus oneself into a scriptural scene—much like an actor "inhabiting" a role or as Atticus Finch suggests in *To Kill a Mockingbird*:

> If you can learn a simple trick, Scout, you'll get along a lot better with all kinds of folks. You never really understand a person until you consider things from his point of view . . . climb into his skin and walk around in it.

Unlike theologians or catechists, we're not here interested in knowing *about* God, but in knowing *God*—just as those Old Testament Bedouins did, just as those fishermen and tax men and whores knew Jesus the Nazarene. Use all the senses, Ignatius suggests. Feel the powdery dust between your own toes in your sandals. Feel the rough-woven fabric of your tunic chafing the skin of your back and shoulders. Smell Jesus' sweat, feel the sandpapery carpenter's calluses on his finger pads and palms, catch the confident twinkle in his eyes when Peter the fumbler makes some outrageous claim.

That is the God I envision when I pray—so it's not like nattering away on the phone, just trusting the other party isn't holding the receiver at arm's length, waiting for me to shut up. It's so much easier than talking across the endless abyss of space to "way out there" where heaven is. Because heaven isn't any distance away. It's closer than my skin. There is nowhere I can evade God's presence (Psalm 139).

When I pray, Jesus and I are bumping along in the cab of his pickup truck. He's a shepherd, you see. Not the wussy, dewy-eyed Good Shepherd of the holy cards who handles only lambs. He's a big guy, like Hugh Jackman, because he also has to wrestle two-hundred-pound stunningly stupid rams up under their armpits with one fist while he clips their wool with the other. And, as Pope Francis so wisely observes, any true shepherd has to smell mightily of sheep. For me, the tang of Jesus truly anchors him.

So there is the kicker. There is a rock-bottom test of your Christian belief. The kickeroo. If you pray, of course you're privileged to share time with God. But are you humble enough to accept in your innermost self that *God* is delighted to share time with *you*?

Ah!

12.

Gratitude

*Good times and bum times, I've seen 'em all
And, my dear, I'm still here.*
—Stephen Sondheim

Gratitude's one of the most difficult virtues. Generosity's actually easier. So are patience, fortitude, even chastity. When we have a firm grip on those virtues, there's a kind of righteous kickback; it says, "See? I'm not such a bad sort after all." But gratitude's, well, a debt, imposed by a kindness emanating from outside ourselves: someone pitching in with the dishes when we're all alone at the sink, someone showing up at the hospital bedside when we really thought suffering alone was more noble, someone bestowing existence on us when we didn't exist and could do nothing to have deserved such an invitation.

When we've been graced, it behooves us to be grace full. Grateful.

But for many people, especially those of us who've been around awhile, gratitude's not an opportunity to rejoice and be more generous, just another word for "indebtedness," and nobody likes bills. Bills have been our stories' antagonists since before we left school. We don't socialize with pawnbrokers and bookies. Debt's a condition we'd just as soon not be reminded of. It makes us feel almost . . . guilty. Best thing to do is just stow that sense of indebtedness in some attic in our minds, and maybe it can become less bothersome. We admit it's real but . . . out of the way.

And yet it's a fact that won't go away. We're all indebted—to our mothers for carrying us around nine months and risking death so we could live, to our fathers for being flinty places against which to hone our adulthood. Who was the teacher who taught us to read, who refused to accept swamp-gas essays? Who reached out to us in our anguish and said, "You're not alone"? And we're indebted to God for . . . everything.

They were all generous to us before we even knew we were in need. In fact, before we even were. And their generosity—even though it was offered with no strings from them—sets up an inescapable obligation within us, provided of course we want to be men and women of honor.

That's bad enough. But it gets worse. Over and above taking life—and all that gift invites us to—for granted, we can't help but gripe that the gift wasn't more . . . unrestricted, more bountiful, less selective in distributing its specialties. "She got wealthier, more educated parents than I did; He got a better set of genes. Look at those muscles. They never have the troubles I do." We spend so much time griping about the accommodations, we never realize how childish it is, sulking because it's someone else's birthday party we were invited to, not our own.

A while ago, I was walking around the campus, just hangin' out with Jesus awhile, when I ran into a young man I'd taught two years before. He said, "You know, I've been meaning to stop around and see you. I've been thinking for a long time that you were the meanest, toughest, most relentless teacher I ever had. . . . And I never thanked you."

Well, I walked away six inches off the ground! For a teacher, gratitude's about as rare as snow in the Sahara. I imagine parents find the same rarity. You just go on, doling out, absorbing the resentment, clinging to the hope that one day Helen Keller's going to understand. You don't do it in order to be thanked. Just because . . . well, you can't help it. It's love.

And yet, paradoxically, a teacher or parent does want to be thanked. Not just because it keeps you going—though God knows it does that. But for the sake of the person you helped, so that they're not the kind of person who takes kindness—even cruel kindness—for granted. So that they become a person ennobled by gratitude.

Surely there's someone you've taken for granted, whom you've never really thanked—even though that person is truly precious to you. Think of that person. The big sister who taught you how to dance, the brother who taught you how to ride a bike, the friend who's absorbed your anger and your frustration and your tears.

Maybe the grammar school nun who held your head while you were sick. Maybe the crusty coach who kept nagging you till you did what you thought you couldn't possibly do. It could even be someone who actually gave you very good advice that you ignored—and now see was the right choice.

Even if that gift giver doesn't expect it, think of the difference it will make in you. That uplift of the soul that is joy.

We're so incredibly spoiled. The very poorest kid in my classes, the kid on third-generation welfare, is luckier than 95 percent of the other kids his age in the whole world. Half the people in the world go to bed hungry, 70 percent can't read, 80 percent are in substandard housing. If you have coins jingling in your pocket, you're rich. If your dinner tonight will be different from last night's, you're breathlessly blessed. The crucial question is whether we're also breathlessly grateful. When I say that, most kids I teach haven't the slightest notion what I'm talking about— even the ones who do service in soup kitchens.

See what I mean? Gratitude makes you very uncomfortable.

What can get rid of it? Just a few lines on a piece of notepaper and the price of a stamp.

Also there's another way. The word "Eucharist" means thanksgiving—not just for good health or material prosperity or lack of tragedy at the moment, but thanks just for the challenge of being born and then for being called to be sons and daughters of the Most High. Can we feel grateful to be entrusted with being the salt of the earth . . . the light set on a lampstand . . . the welcoming hands of the promiscuous Christ?

You can't feel thankful if you're spoiled, if you take it all for granted. Who's grateful for peristalsis, respiration, binocular vision? How often do we feel a surge of blessedness when we ponder our spouses, our kids, our friends? As Chesterton says, people sometimes ask whom to thank for the presents in their stockings Christmas morning. But they rarely think to thank someone for putting legs into the stockings they put on every day.

On the one hand, we've been pretty spoiled with more than anyone needs of the world's goods, and on the other, we've been pretty impoverished of the exhilaration of the gospel's invitation to stand up and be counted—to write a letter to the editor, to tell someone on the parish council that the homilies are a test of our faith, to sit with the one who always sits alone in the cafeteria? *Noblesse oblige.*

Again, when you feel shortchanged by life, sit down with a piece of paper and list all the things you love: mountains at sunrise, star-strewn summer nights. It'll take quite a while, I'm pretty sure. When you're finished, try to thank God for inviting you into all that.

It won't enrich God very much, but it'll sure enrich you.

i thank You God for most this amazing day.

—e. e. cummings

13.
Empathy

*Kinship. At the edges, we join the easily despised
and the readily left out. We stand with the
demonized so that the demonizing will stop.
We situate ourselves right next to the disposable
so that the day will come when we stop throwing
people away.*
— Gregory Boyle, S.J.

Every year when we ponder in ethics class what being part of a
family means, I show Robert Redford's film *Ordinary People*. I've
seen it now probably about thirty times, but every time I switch
the CD off at the end, after the son has finally been able to tell his
father he loves him, and the father has told him he loves him, too,
I always end up with tears in my eyes. So one year, I mentioned
that, and from the class (all boys) came mock groans and hoots of
"Awww!" Apparently, to feel deeply for a stranger—or at least to
show it or admit it—is very uncool.

I pulled myself up to my inconsiderable height and glared. "You
guys really *scare me*, you know that?" They sobered up pretty fast.
"Are your self-defenses so strong you can't even allow yourself at
least a bit of fellow feeling for a man and a boy whose wife and
mother have just walked out on them, who just cling together in
shared pain?" One kid sneered, "Well, you can feel sorry for somebody without breaking down in *sobs.*" Exaggerating my reaction so
he could reduce it to something absurd, and therefore not have to
censor his own callousness in any way.

What bothered me was the need of so many of them to mock
genuine sentiment, honest fellow feeling. Then I began to wonder
if their seeming hard-heartedness was only one small part in a kind
of "general defensiveness" that's almost essential today, at least in
big, overcrowded, noisy, dangerous cities. Locking oneself inside

an iPod is another way to block out the chaos. Walking corridors and sidewalks with invisible blinders is another. Focus on the subway ads and on the elevator numbers rather than "sharing" the space with the others who are there but in no really meaningful (inconvenient, intrusive, even hurtful) way. If you refuse to notice them, they may not go away, but they'll become less real. There's just so much one can deal with; if you let in all the stimuli, you'd blow all your mental circuits. Best to zip up the old cocoon and let the rest of the world roll by, unnoticed and incapable of upsetting.

Television and films have a similar effect. By the time little kids hit kindergarten, they've seen more deaths—real or fictional—than a veteran in the army of Julius Caesar, to the point that psychiatrists say they can't tell the difference between real pain and acted pain. A great many of the blockbuster movies bristle with explosions and mayhem until those scenes are no more able to move—or shock—anyone than the explosions in a videogame. On the other hand, we're also besieged with public service announcements showing African children with great glistening, mournful eyes, flies drinking up their tears, making us feel helplessly soul bruised, to the point where it just becomes too much. We flick the dial, turn the page, render ourselves amnesiac about it. It's just too much overload for anyone to cope with.

That general "soul numbing" is understandable. But also impoverishing. At the core of *Ordinary People* is the need of the mother, Beth, and the son, Conrad, to have "control." The elder brother, Buck, died in a boating accident. At Buck's funeral, Beth and Conrad were the only ones who didn't cry. They couldn't allow themselves to. And Conrad felt such inexpressible guilt at having survived the accident that he attempted suicide. The father, Calvin, reaches out to both of them, but they can't allow him access to their pain, nor can they allow themselves to identify with his pain. But as Burger, the psychiatrist in the film, says, "If you can't feel pain . . . you won't feel anything else either." The cocoon may very well be protective, but it's also very small and smothering.

Empathy, sympathy, compassion. Different words, but made up of similar parts: em-, sym-, and com- are Greek and Latin roots meaning "with." "Path" and "passion" mean "suffer." So all three words mean "to suffer with." They denote a reality inside a person that *resonates* with the anguish inside another human being, *identifies* with it. In a sense, they're all "victim" words, and since few of us court victimhood, they can be scary even to consider. Empathy, sympathy, and compassion go far beyond what my uneasy student meant by "feeling sorry for," a pity that can be very remote, chilly, only slightly warmer than indifference. It also goes beyond respect, which we can honestly offer to another person without any personal involvement or cost. Respect is the first step on the road to justice; empathy is the first step on the road to love.

Probably no one of us doesn't want to love and be loved—or at least we claim we do. And yet, if we genuinely want the goal and we are honest with ourselves, we also must genuinely want the *means* to the goal. For instance, if I claim to want an education, that should be evident in what I do, large and small, from putting in a full forty-hour week to writing outlines. Without that concrete evidence, my claim is a lie I tell myself—and worse—believe.

The same is true of loving. If I claim (even in just an unspoken way within myself) to be a loving person, I should be able to be "convicted" of that by my concrete behavior and responses. If I claim to love my parents, that claim is undercut if I grouse when asked to take out the trash, refuse to be truthful with them, deny them an honest day's work for an honest day's pay. I might like to *think* I love them, but my actions prove pretty convincingly I'm lying—to myself. If I love my parents, truly, there's no way I could possibly be "too busy" or "forget" to call. Real loving costs. If it doesn't, using the word "love" is a self-delusion.

Similarly, we can be stingy with our love, restricting it in a very unloving way to a very narrow, insulated group, which is also self-impoverishing. If what makes humans different from animals is that we can keep learning and loving, then the more things we learn and the more people we love, the more our lives—our *selves*—are enriched. The only obstacle to that enrichment is our own fears about being "taken in," hoaxed, made to look foolish. But if you never let yourself be taken in, you'll never see the inside of anything.

Nine times out of ten, when you offer someone your trust, that person will honor your trust. The same thing is true of offering your empathy for another's suffering; it enriches not only the receiver but the giver. True enough, one time out of ten you'll offer your trust to someone and get scorched. We all have the scars to prove that. But to avoid that one scorching, we give up those nine potential friends, even though everything about them seems to indicate they can in fact be trusted. "Better safe than sorry." And when you allow yourself honestly to be moved by someone else's anguish, you risk being laughed at, as my class laughed at me. But do English teachers ever tell kids the reason they read novels is to develop empathy? Do we learn our kinship with strangers solely by accident? The second Christian commandment says we ought to love them, but does anybody show us how to begin? I'd rather be laughed at by a group of tough-souled boys than become a tough-souled old man to achieve their dubious approval.

Take the case of the panhandler. No person reading this page hasn't been ambushed by at least a few. The standard, practical response is to divert your attention and pass them by. They're almost certainly going to spend whatever you give on booze or drugs, right, especially if they're disheveled and smell bad? You can almost convince yourself you're doing them a *kindness* by denying them help. But just for a moment, remember what Atticus Finch suggests in *To Kill a Mockingbird:* get inside their skin and walk around in it awhile. How did this person get where he is now? Quite likely he or she wasn't always this way. Would anyone really *want* to surrender dignity, self-esteem, to put out their paw and beg from strangers? And looking at it from a broader perspective, what's he asking for? Less than the cost of a single telephone call. (You can see why gratitude came before empathy, right?)

If you sincerely want to be a caring person and you're honestly afraid this money they ask for food is really going for drugs, buy them a sandwich or a banana. If (as can happen) they sneer at that gift and really are phony, *you'll* at least have proven that you're *not*. The question here really isn't whether the beggar is in authentic need but whether you're authentically kind. Personally, I'd rather be bilked by nine beggars in a row than pass by the tenth who was really needy. And if you give someone a gift certificate at Christmas, do you often say, "Now, be sure to buy something I'd approve of, right?"

The first step toward the empathy that enriches both receiver and giver is to *notice* them. Granted, if you don't notice them, they're less likely to cause you grief. But not noticing guarantees they'll never become your friend. When I walk through the corridors, I purposely try to focus on as many faces as I can out of the chaos of class changes. I never once have done it without seeing someone who, by their build, must be at least a junior, and I've never noticed them before. Whenever I cross the university campus, I try to catch eyes with everybody I pass and say, "Hi," and almost invariably they say, "Hi," back. Small thing, but a start. And it's a lot less lonely.

Volunteering is another way to get your empathetic juices stirring. All of us know the queasy reluctance we feel visiting someone in a hospital or a nursing home, the same aversion most people feel at the outset of their first service project: "Those old people will smell, and they'll paw me and make me feel awful. Those handicapped kids will drool and won't understand and fight me off." But I've rarely seen anyone who sincerely tried a service project who didn't come back saying, "I went to give them something and, without my even realizing till now, they were giving *me* something. Something important." A sense that you're not negligible, that you can in fact make a difference, a small difference maybe, but a meaningful one.

As for all those painful pictures of needy children, we can avert our eyes from them, too, refuse to notice them, but again in denying them we are denying ourselves. Take just one fact about them: UNICEF reports that each *day* one thousand children go blind because they have no access to twenty cents worth of Vitamin A; even if they did, their parents couldn't afford it. Think of that. For the cost of one compact disc, I could save *sixty-five* kids from lifelong blindness! You can't crusade for all of even the worthiest causes, but to be a person of character, you ought to choose just *one*.

Yet another way of developing a sense of humanity (character) is simply to go through your closet and drawers and pick out anything you haven't worn in a year. Obviously, you have no remote need of it, and it could save someone's life—or at least give them a momentary lift. And even in a worst-case scenario, where the Salvation Army driver steals all the best stuff and fences it for money—in the first place, you'll never know that, and in the second place, your compassion and generosity have done something very good inside *you*.

Novels, plays, and films can help evolve our empathetic powers, too—if we're not too well defended against them. *Shane, The Elephant Man, A Man for All Seasons, Death of a Salesman, Our Town*—all written by great souls capable of reaching down into the human heart and coming back with something that speaks to our own hearts, if they're open. From a play whose name I can't remember comes a line I can never forget: "Coward, take my coward's hand." That says what true empathy is.

Finally, empathy helps to develop the very humanizing virtue of forgiveness. If anyone has pesky, intrusive kids around, it's easy to fly off the handle at them. Especially if they're not your own, thus imperfectly brought up. Try to get into their skins, try to remember what it was like when you were their age—confused, feeling left out, not quite understanding, self-centered—in fact, lacking precisely the virtue we're exploring here: empathy. When a parent snaps or overreacts, the other parent ought to ask kids to see the parent's reactions from the inside, rather than just from their own (quite limited) point of view. "Someday, you'll probably be a parent yourself. How would you act differently? Or would you?"

Many people sneer that empathy is a "sucker" virtue, and it surely is. Yet all of us want to believe our lives are in some way useful. Yet to be useful, we have to be used.

14.
Kindness

*The unfortunate need people who will be kind
to them. The prosperous need people to whom to
be kind.*

—Aristotle

The first week of September 1997, everyone's life overflowed with pictures of a serenely beautiful young woman unselfconsciously kneeling at the feet of AIDS patients, or arms comfortably wrapped round a Bosnian girl whose legs had been blown off by a landmine, or fondling a dark baby gazing up in awe at this flawless white face. There were also pictures of a tiny, wrinkled old nun, her face radiating tranquility, doing essentially the same things: cuddling infants, consoling lepers, easing the final journey of the dying.

There couldn't have been two more different faces, the one youthful and satin skinned, the other age-worn and leathery as a purse. Their backgrounds could not have been more different, the one a woman of rank and privilege, the other a woman who'd vowed away all money to care for lepers in the gutters of Calcutta. Yet each shared that physical and psychological ease with broken bodies and spirits, each radiated a glow of genuine caring that touched hearts all over the world and made them genuinely mourn the two women's deaths within the same week. And I found myself saying, "What a wonderful aura unaffected kindness gives to a face."

Charity and courtesy can be faked; kindness can't. Witness the contrast, on the one hand, between idly (or grimly) dropping a coin in a beggar's cup or a waiter's smarmy fawning and on the other, the natural, motherly ease of Princess Diana of Wales and Mother Teresa of Calcutta caressing hurt children and the awed acceptance of their kindness in the children's eyes.

Whenever I ask students what makes "a really good friend," they often answer that a good friend is someone you can count on to "be there" when you're in need. That's pretty vague. When you're in pain, confused, hurt, lost, the walls of your room are "there," but not very heartening. Your old faithful dog could be "there," too, and even whimper in empathy, but she's no real consolation. When a good friend is "there" for you, it means you can *feel* their empathy, even if they can't "solve" your problem with words. At a wake, when there's nothing anyone can say to make the pain of loss go away, a friend can only put his or her arms around you, and that touch says, "I'm here with you. I don't know what to do either. But you're not alone." Families or friends who have a barrier against touch and tears will find their mutual life far more difficult than families more comfortable with physical vulnerability.

Touch seems much easier for girls than for boys, and certainly easier for mature women than for men. Surely part of the reason is from *nurture*, from the way we're brought up. People just "expect" young girls to be more caring, to play with dolls like little mothers, to grow up to be nurses or teachers. They also accept the male stereotype that boys never cry, never show tenderness, and surely never, never touch anyone, especially another male. Okay to have a huge group hug when you've scored the winning goal, but in any other situation . . . well, you don't want to give anybody the idea you're queer, right? There also seems some unwritten law that, when a boy gets into the later years of grade school, fathers have to stop touching them, and even if a genuinely loving father wants to show real physical affection for his sons, the sons repel it. Again, okay to roughhouse but not to caress.

They are stifling stereotypes, smothering girls' natural human impulse to challenge and boys' human impulse to share compassion, neither likely to go away. All one hopes is that some adult mentor can convince young people how truly stupid and impoverishing the stereotypes are.

But another reason females are more comfortable with touch roots itself, I think, in *nature*, from the physical way we are made. Psychologists believe that, because girls grow up (usually) with a person of their own sex, they define themselves and acceptable behavior by bonding with their mothers, while boys who grow up (usually) with a person of the opposite sex define themselves and acceptable behavior by separation from the mother, setting up psychological and physical ego boundaries. Also, they find that, even before stereotypes can be drummed into them by media and peers, girls building scenes with blocks and human figures build almost exclusively warm, inclusive interiors with welcoming doorways, while boys almost exclusively build exteriors with turrets and defensive battlements, and ruins occur only in boys' constructs. Girls at least *seem* by nature more inclusive, boys more resistant to enclosure.

The only objective difference between males and females is genital, girls with interior genitals and boys with exterior genitals. Other than that, females and males are absolutely equal and deserve equal treatment. But although they're equal, they are not the *same*, any more than a cow is a bull or a mare is a stallion. Both males and females are intelligent beings, but they are also *embodied* beings, and the body does have an effect on one's psychology, one's attitudes, one's view of the self and the world. Skin color, loss of a limb, a wasting disease have a stunning impact on the mind and soul, but they do not make us less human. Often, in fact, they have precisely the opposite effect. But the body does alter a person's viewpoint.

The same, I think, must be true of our physical sexual differences. I cannot help but think that, by nature and not by custom, females and males view life from different angles—not unequal, mind you, just different. I cannot believe there is not a marked psychological difference between a person who has accustomed herself to the monthly bleeding of menstruation and a male who has not. There must be a difference in her sensitivity to pain and to her compassion for others who undergo suffering. (This does not mean only women would make good nurses, but it does imply they might be naturally better at it—and perhaps better at being doctors, too.) Far more, I cannot believe a woman who has actually conceived, carried, nursed, cared for, cleaned, fed, and coddled even a single child would not be profoundly affected by those experiences, and sensitized in a way no male—no matter how well intentioned— could ever be. All women don't react either to menstruation or to childbearing in the same way. But no man has ever had even the opportunity.

There are probably some females reading these pages who do, in fact, need a bit of "softening up," putting *down* their defenses against openheartedness, openhandedness, reaching out to touch someone in need. But my educated hunch tells me there are far more males who need it. The women's movement has made giant strides in convincing males sexual stereotypes are not only insulting to women but also psychologically impoverishing to men. More men nowadays share tasks simpler-minded ages restricted exclusively to females (if not slaves): cooking, cleaning, diapering, and so forth. It's now a staple of advertisements to see a hunk with his infant asleep on his bare chest. And every male should be grateful for that liberation to be a fully human being—and fully male.

But what would be a "typical" father's response to his son's shame-faced admission that he had gotten his girlfriend pregnant? (1) rail and curse, threaten, abuse; (2) offer "the" answer "This is what we're going to do, young man"; (3) collapse into a swamp of self-recrimination—"How have I failed?"; or (4) put his arms around him and grieve with him. That's the test of genuine love: "For the moment, your shame is more important than the shame you've brought on me." To repeat, the family uncomfortable with touch will have a harder time facing life.

Often, the only way to elicit a sense of fellow feeling strong enough to overcome our fear of reaching out is to generate situations that will make people *feel* their lack of it and how mean spirited and impoverished their lives are without it. I start off a class on prejudice asking someone to describe a bigot (Archie Bunker used to be handy for that, but we'll never lack for them: "Never go broke betting on dumb."). They wade in gleefully, talking about impregnable dogmatism, certitudes about blacks, Poles, Jews, Cat'licks, based on hearsay without a shred of objective evidence. We can laugh because we consider ourselves open minded, live and let live.

Then I snap the trap. Okay, then what about overweight girls with glasses at a dance? Open minded about them? Unprejudiced? (Snickers.) How about unathletic boys? Did you ever think of saying, "You mind if I show you how you can throw that better"? (Embarrassed shrugs.) Then the kicker: How about homosexuals? (Cold, stiff-faced silence.) "If you're looking for a bigot, don't turn around. One's sitting inside your head." That's not restricted to kids.

I admit I was exactly the same at their age. I came home one day in my senior year, and my mother informed me I was escorting Sylvie Smith to her senior prom. Sylvie lived in the neighborhood; I'd gone to grade school with her. She was pale as a peeled potato, with frizzy red hair and granny glasses, and there wasn't a curve on her body I could discern. So of course I informed my mother I was most certainly *not* going to squire Sylvie to her ball.

Backstory: This to a woman who, when I skipped a piano lesson to go to the Saturday kids' matinee (two features, two serials, cartoons), appeared in the back of the packed theater hollering, "Where are you, Bill O'Malley? I know you're there." Then, muttering about spending good money on those lessons, she strode down the aisle, into the row, and hauled me by the ear through five hundred hooting kids out into the harsh light of reality.

Thus, it goes without saying that I did, indeed, escort Sylvie to her ball.

By now the students are really guffawing: "Ol' Hotshot O'Malley!" And it got worse. I didn't have my night driving license. So my *dad* had to *drive* us. (Belly laughs.) And it got worse. We got there on *time* so we were—desolately—alone together. I tried every conversation ploy I could think of, just short of the causes of the First World War. Nothing. And it got worse. My *pals* started to arrive, elbowing one another, snickering. Besides all that, I am one world-class dancer; Sylvie, alas, was not. The shine was gone from my shoes within minutes. So about eleven-thirty I said, "Well, it's getting late," so I called my dad and we took her home.

They're hooting! Then I say, very quietly, "What a selfish sonofabitch I was."

Dead silence. Suddenly, they *feel* it. They understand.

It was her first date, her first formal dress, her first night out from a very rigid family. And for three hours, I had thought of nothing but myself. The kids are really with me now. Because they've been there themselves. What would happen, I ask, if you went up to an unattractive girl and asked her to dance? What would it take? Fifteen minutes of your life? And she'd go home thinking, "Hey, maybe I'm *not* the Miss Godzilla after all!"

After all these years, I can anticipate their objections: she'd think it was a trick, condescending; my pals would think I was an idiot; she'd become a leech on the phone all the time. All of which misses the point: You'd have made someone happy. You'd have been kind.

We have enormous power: to give life or give living death, but most of us are unaware of the effect we can have on other people by our kindness or by our cutting remarks. This lesson doesn't have the same effect on students as Helen Keller's encounter with the pump, when her whole idea of life exploded, but it is a definite crack in the defenses.

If you've had kids of your own, or if you've been privileged to teach them, you have to have ingested the helpless urge to "forgive" those who've been shortchanged by life, which is the prerequisite of learning the kindness skills. They're skills unappreciated in "the dog-eat-dog world" where humanity gets ground under by The Beast. There's something to be said in favor of letting a child who's run afoul of the law, say, driving impaired, stew in the lockup a few hours. But then there has to be forgiveness, open arms. Or else parents have to stop calling themselves Christian. Because "Christian" boils down to two words: "forgiveness" and "resurrection."

If the "law" of "the jungle" has been the moral matrix of the forty-hour work week that gave your life sustenance, shape, and meaning—and goals and values—for your entire adulthood, isn't it about time you got honest perspective on it? Isn't it time to crack open your horizons to the infinite dimensions of The Really Real? To see that how the "weight" of all values shifts seismically when you move everything from this reality into that reality? In the trust sense, the values of the world become weightless as astronauts in a space capsule.

Contrarily, the only currency that qualifies for entrance to the Kingdom are values the world finds "airy, unsubstantial, lightweight." St. Paul describes them as the fruits of the Holy Spirit: "love, joy, peace, patience, kindness, decency, faithfulness, gentleness and self-control" (Galatians 5:22–23). Those tokens answer the only question asked at the border: "Lord, when was it that we saw you hungry and gave you food, or thirsty and gave you something to drink? And when was it that we saw you a stranger and welcomed you, or naked and gave you clothing? And when was it that we saw you sick or in prison and visited you?" (Matthew 25: 37–38).

If you've lost those, you still have time to work on your Kingdom credentials.

In Kurt Vonnegut's *God Bless You, Mr. Rosewater*, a woman asks a gentle, generous eccentric to give her child a commandment to live by, and he says, "There's only one commandment: Goddammit, you've got to be kind."

15.
Loving

Love never quits.

—1 Corinthians 13:8

Think of ancient dollar bills. Limp and fragile as dead flower petals. The word "love" is just as frayed. More than any other word in the language, just ahead of "value," it's overused and mishandled. First, we use it routinely for less than people: "I love your diamond; I love pizza; my dog loves me." The same word we use about our mothers, spouses, children. Second, too many use the word for people but in a way that truly debases the word, as when TV dramas and pop songs say "making love" when they mean no more than release of sexual tension. Third, we use "love" when what we really mean is need, infatuation, romance. A wonderful experience, but it's not the undiluted reality that encompasses the love of a mother in labor, a father saying, "Go back to sleep. I'll change her." The other day a college student said in class, "I just realized something. What I always thought love meant is what you call 'being in love.'" And fourth, there's times we wonder whether the word might also be misused in a different, tissue-thin way, as in, "Love God with your whole soul, and love your neighbor just as you love yourself."

Maybe I can help disentangle all those uses by positing a thesis (a Pop Warner Aquinas) and trying to establish its truth.

Thesis: genuine love is not (essentially) a feeling. Love is an act of the will, commitment that takes over when the feelings *fail*, when the one loved hasn't been even likable for a while.

Real love—unlike feeling love—is undramatic, every day, commonplace. It's the touchstone to judge every other love. Two spouses who've faced pregnancies and unpayable bills and still say, "I'd rather be unhappy with you than happy with someone else." Parents when they punish kids: "I love you enough I can put up with your hating me awhile for this, as long as you don't get hurt." The key to genuine love is that the other comes first, before oneself.

My dictionary has thirty-three lines defining love, and when I finished, I said, "I wish I knew as little about love as that Noah Webster did." In *Fiddler on the Roof*, Golde does better than define love: "For twenty-five years I've lived with him, fought with him, starved with him. Twenty-five years my bed is his. If that's not love, what is?" Another example came from someone less experienced but no less wise. A seventeen-year-old boy was head over heels for a girl, but she began to take an interest in one of his friends. He told me later, in tears, that he'd told her, "If you think he can make you happier than I can, that's what I want."

Both of those lack the full-throttle, operatic grandeur of Antony and Cleopatra, but they're the real thing. When the honeymoon's over and the being-in-love fades, that's when the loving has to start—the very undramatic but very real commitment to put up with one another's shortcomings (which didn't even exist while they were in love), with sharing diapers and bills and foul moods. I don't like the kids who do the absolute minimum for a diploma, but I love them enough to badger and flunk them, even if they hate me for it. That's love.

Most of us looking back at age forty have long since learned Tristan and Isolde, Romeo and Juliet, and Maria and Tony didn't really love one another but were pixilated with love potion. In fact, they've yet to learn you can't *make* anyone love you, or love you more than he or she is able, or in the way you hoped. Now, loving's hurt us enough—and still been worth trying again, that we know if what you call "love" doesn't cost, you're using the wrong word. Love hasn't hurt teenagers enough yet for them to discern the real thing through the haze of romance.

Romance, what even college kids mean by love, is what H. L. Mencken meant when he said, "Love is the triumph of imagination over intelligence."

The meaning of the word "love" has been built up not by calm philosophical reflection but by films and song lyrics, relentlessly conditioning our values as effectively as commercials. They brainwashed us to believe love has to do with affection, fibrillations, the anguish of jealousy, sexual tension. Nope. Other animals feel those, though only a few times a year at most, while we fall victim to it more often than junkies for a fix—with the same hope. Anesthesia. The more love involves any kind of kickback, the more slippery the label becomes. As much as I love my dog, my dog's incapable of loving me. In honesty, I have to confess dogs have genuine affection, but they haven't the wherewithal to differentiate love from need, any more than they can separate making love from copulation. The acid test: If faced with saving an infant or a puppy, I have to go with the human baby. No other animal can make that distinction.

Nor, clearly, can one use "making love" for casual uncommitted sex. No matter what anyone asserts about it, human sex is not—in itself—the same as animal sex. Both are physical, but human sex has a psychological element that can't justly be denied. As far as we know, no orangutan kills herself because her mate is getting it on with her girlfriends. Humans do. Human sex makes a "statement." You can't be more vulnerable than in that physical situation—more defenseless than you've been with your own parents or physicians. The sex may be exhilarating, but it's a lie, not loving.

The problem gets abrasive when the psychological element is, indeed, involved—as it is in romance. In my lifetime embedded like a war correspondent with young people, I've been constantly frustrated trying to convince newcomers to adulthood there's a difference. But the most successful test is "by their fruits you shall know them." Especially when there's a strong sexual element, does it make both partners more open *outside* the relationship? More joyful, spirited, open, sensitive to others' needs as they are to the loved ones? Or does it make them more thin-skinned, underhanded, devious? When I ask that in class, many look rightfully abashed.

Some kids going steady are more exclusive and monogamous—and stifling—than most marriages. They have this unwritten-but-very-heavy agreement he won't have significant friends of her sex and she won't have any meaningful friends of his sex. And they tell themselves they love one another. Crazy. If he sees her talking pretty heavily alone with some guy, he seethes; if she sees him having a great laugh with a girl, she goes into howling laments worthy of Medea. Don't call that love. Call it by its right name: possessiveness, slavery.

The first step toward wisdom—and freedom—is to call a thing by its true name. There's a real difference between genuine love and romance: being in love. And there's a real parallel between being in love and chemical addiction. First of all, you can't think of anything else. And you can't get enough of it. When you've got it, God's in his heaven and all's right with the world. You take temporary leave of everyday so-called reality, and when you've got your fix, you're no longer bound by the laws that bind ordinary people—even gravity! You're flying.

Don't get me wrong. Nothing wrong with being in love. A totally splendiferous feeling, and anyone who gets through life without having been swamped by it, enthralled by it, steam-rollered by it, is surely impoverished. In fact, the heady wine of romance is absolutely essential. Who'd dare get up in front of hundreds of people at a wedding and vow responsibility for another person, in sickness and in health, *no matter what,* till death do us part, without being a bit intoxicated? Being in love's a wonderful place to visit. But few can live there long. Reality takes over. There's nothing wrong with being in love—just in confusing it with the real thing.

At the far end of the spectrum, some good people wonder if it's too much of a stretch to use love for the neighbor and for God. Unarguable that the feelings most people unthinkingly mean by "love" simply can't bear the strain. Because it's the wrong word! Lazy, incautious word choice. If I'm right, and you can legitimately use the word "love" for people you don't like, then you can use the word even for people you don't *know.*

If that seems mere semantic snobbishness, crack the thesaurus and see that a treasury of words expresses a true "act of the will that takes over when the feelings fail." In the index of this so-precious book, omitting the four umbrella entries "affection, gods of love, liking, and sexuality" (which risk kickback), there are eight more inclusive headings: "accord, beloved, benevolence, endearment, friendship, regards, virtue"—all of which denote an outward-looking concern. And each of those tags refers to pages and pages of other precisions.

I wonder, if we could train ourselves to use words with respect and caution, there might be fewer broken hearts, suicides, drive-in marriages, quickie divorces. All that memorizing of word lists for the SATs has been trivialized as a narrow gate to solvency, when the first step toward wisdom is to call anything by its right name. A silly suggestion of course, like dropping frozen foods on our enemies instead of bombs.

Genuine love is a spectrum, not a dualistic either/or. There are the billions of anonymous people out there I truly love—not with the same *intensity* as for my best friends, but it's truly love. If I had fifty bucks, I'd rather send it to Covenant House to take care of teen prostitutes or to keep African babies from going blind than to take myself to dinner—or save whales.

Then there are acquaintances; I genuinely love them, even if, at times, I don't find them attractive—not a feeling; an act of the will. In fact, that love might reveal sensitivity more honestly than loving those I feel easy affection for. Am I capable of the love Jesus asked for the hardly known neighbor. "If all you do is love the lovable, do you expect a bonus? Anybody can do that" (Matthew 5:46 MSG). I give them the tribute of my courtesy, even when—especially when—they don't deserve it. On the shadow side, I will *not* degrade them, nor will I stand by while someone else treats them with less than their due dignity. But if I'm groping beyond humanity to ignite the light of Christ, I'll try to be as attentive to their faces as I am to my own when I shave. I'll have the courage (and confidence) to say, "I don't want to intrude, but are you okay?" That qualifies as love, I think, because it costs me—attention, empathy, kindness—plus shedding reserve, which many find as threatening as black ice.

Then there are friends, not pals, but people you'd feel comfortable with in the cafeteria. None of your conversations deserves to be recorded, but there's genuine affection, watchfulness, concern. Beneath the chit-chat, there's a deeper conversation going on that says, "I care about you." If anyone in the group had a wallet stolen, all the other wallets would be out. If you're in the hospital, they'll be there. You might not be invited to the reception but you will be to the wedding. And that readiness is a gift of self, an act of love, surely.

Then there are pals, your gang, the people you just assume you're going to the cafeteria with—and the reception, and the funeral. They're the people—sadly—you take for granted, people you truly, genuinely love—if "love" has any meaning at all. I say "sadly" because it'd be such a wonderful gift to hear it said, just once: "Ahem, I, uh, love you." We all want to hear it. Sad that our shy self-protectiveness never allows us to say it. Even very often to our own parents, who've loved us since before we had faces—and long, long before they ever saw our faces. Tactfulness is so inhibiting and sometimes even stupid.

Finally, best friends, people we'd stand up and be counted for, bail out, weep with, who'll tell us boldly when we're making asses of ourselves or misusing booze or money or those we love. More precious than anything we envy the American Dream medalists for. Too bad that, in the hurly-burly, we forget that. Too bad we haven't time to pause and reflect on those names, those faces, the people we love—to understand how gifted we are.

Oddly, we learn to love God just as we learn to love one another. First, we've got to notice God, focus on him out of the smear of anonymous faces, make him an acquaintance. Then take him for a long walk, just the two of you, and give him the time and talk it takes to become a friend, a pal, a persnickety, unpredictable, high-handed, desolatingly loyal friend. He's ready. Whenever you are.

How do we love God? By yielding. Letting God be God, accepting the world as God made it, humbling ourselves to accept things as they are. I don't mean Islamic enslavement to the will of Allah, which says that, if Allah made me a slave or a woman, I must surrender and be exploited. That contradicts the will of God we find in evolution, in our own curiosity, in resurrection. I mean the yielding that's due to good spouses and parents: telling God that his unreadable purposes are more important than mine. "Thy will be done." That's love.

Two perniciously subtle forms of blasphemy (trying to grab God's place) are perfectionism and its twin, the demand for certitude. Perfectionism isn't content with good enough; it's always agonizing because you didn't give 110 percent. Nope. You have only 100 percent, and that's quite good enough. Everything you do will be at least slightly imperfect. Accept that; that's what loving God means—imperfectly. And the demand for certitude is not only blasphemous but as frustrating as perfectionism. Only God has certitude. Every answer you ever find, to whatever question, will always need fine-tuning later on. Be content with that. God made us imperfect, so that we could grow.

The hardest God-love is forgiving God—for *being* God, for having reasons we're as yet incapable of fathoming. In fact, forgiveness might be the infallible touchstone of genuine love—in the marriage, the family, at work, in the neighborhood. It might even work in the world.

The father of the prodigal is a model of genuine loving—in a more everyday way than the epic love of the crucifixion, love the way Jesus habitually treated sinners (especially sexual sinners), and the way—one assumes—God intended us to treat one another, especially our own children. All these years we've so incautiously said, "Forgive us our trespasses only *insofar* as we forgive those who trespass against us." Especially those we love most, who can hurt us most.

St. Paul nailed it. "Love is always patient and kind. It's never jealous. Love is never boastful or conceited. It's never rude, or selfish, or quick to take offense, or resentful. Love takes no pleasure in other people's faults but delights only in the truth. Love is always ready to forgive, to trust, to hope. Love never quits" (1 Corinthians 13:8).

16.
Curiosity

Face it. Curiosity
will not cause us to die—
only lack of it will.

—Alistair Reed

In the subway car, a little girl sits, docile but alert, her pacifier working unheeded but essential in her silken, café-au-lait cheeks. Her sparrow eyes dart about, scrounging. I catch her attention and make a goopy face, and hers crinkles back. Then her eyes flutter upward to her left, catching the man nodding overhead toward her mother's shoulder, spaced on something, perhaps only fatigue, a thin line of drool lingering at the edge of his mouth. Her mother's face sags, eyes fixed on nowhere, dulled with disillusion, if not despair. The only thing solid in her life seems the small brown-eyed bundle clutched in her parched hands. The baby peers back and forth at the other faces nodding numbly all round her, as if in servile acceptance of the task of merely surviving. She doesn't know she's studying her future.

Everyone in that car was like her once. What got lost?

More often than not, I fear, people sort of "drop out," settle for a "realistic" acceptance of what seems irresistibly "the way things are." They adjust to the humdrum, even to the antihuman, which then becomes the norm, the cramping we share with everybody else. And after a while we don't even notice how impoverished we've become.

Children, like all genuine philosophers, are born mentally and sensorily ravenous. Every child-care expert exhorts parents to feed that hunger every moment the child is awake: goo-goo eyes, senseless prattle, singing, patting, brightly colored toys that make tiny noises. Without such constant stimulation, neurons and synapses in the child's brain literally atrophy, incapable of rejuvenation. A part of the physical brain in fact dies. In their first years, well-nurtured children ingest a larger body of new information than they'll assimilate in all their formal schooling. It's difficult to assess how much mental damage occurs in an infant when his or her mother returns to work a few weeks after the child's birth, turned over—however reluctantly—to people who might be caring but who are responsible for many children at once.

I think the death of curiosity begins sometime in second grade. Up till then, a child's life has been a fascinating odyssey: "All experience is an arch wherethrough gleams that untraveled world, whose margin fades for ever and for ever when I move." There are the constant stimuli from eager parents, intriguing stories experienced in the security of an adult lap, then puzzles and games, *Sponge Bob* and *Sesame Street*, inventive play with other children, turning boxes into turrets and mud into bagels. For most children, preschool, kindergarten, and even first grade are stimulating: "Look, Mommy! I can write my own name! See?"

Then around second grade, "the system" takes over. Life's a serious business. Time to get efficient and serious. SATs! The purpose of schooling is to prepare children for "the real world," and that means developing the verbal and computational skills to make them attractive job candidates. Even the humanities fall victim to those grad-grind goals. English, for instance, must resolutely focus on memorizing vocabulary from lists rather than developing an addiction to books and words from kindergarten on. Even poetry isn't to move the soul but analysis fodder: separating a simile from a metaphor (as if that mattered more than the delight in recognizing and making them!) and to point out where the poet uses alliteration (without the slightest sense of the emotive effect the poet intended). An iron syllabus and lesson plans become more important than judging whether children's minds and hearts and souls are still growing.

Every time I say that to college students, they chuckle, knowingly, nostalgically. As Einstein said, "It's a miracle curiosity survives formal education."

Specifically human life begins to die when we stop asking "why." Children begin to feel it's somehow impolite to be too inquisitive. Teachers and parents actually worry if a child might suffer some mental aberration if he or she keeps pestering, badgering, asking unsettling questions, intruding on the lesson plan—even though that's what learning (as opposed to schooling) is all about. Plato, who seemed to know a great deal about being human, thought no doctrine more important than simply keeping talking, asking questions. By the time we reach thirty, our bodies have gotten just about as good as they can get; in fact, they begin to deteriorate slowly. But there's no *natural* limit to the growth and development of the mind and soul. The limit comes only from the inertia we share with the beasts our nature invites us to surpass. From what I've gathered from fifty years of fighting that inertia, I suspect the beast in us wins nine times out of ten. Check out any subway car, any study hall, any corner bar.

Animals can know and communicate facts ("Run, Bambi!"), but as far as we can tell, no animal can ask why, try to comprehend a *reason* for the hunter's lack of empathy, hope to find some unifying meaning within life's hurly-burly. Yet because our learning has constricted from an attempt to comprehend to an attempt to ingest more and more information, we reduce ourselves back to that same primitive level: information rather than understanding. An alien visitor might suspect our school system was training young people for lives playing Trivial Pursuit or appearing on *Jeopardy*. For that same reason, after schooling, our human hunger to know restrains itself to garnering evanescent facts—the seven o'clock news, the sports stats, *People*, weather predictions, the *National Enquirer*, just so we won't appear witless at the water cooler or cocktail parties. Do we need any more proof of general bastardization of curiosity than *Jersey Shore*, *Survivor*, Lindsay Lohan, and Charlie Sheen?

What separates us from other animals is we can learn, and love, and keep growing more fully human, the more learning and loving we do. No wolf can become more vulpine, but it's unchallengeable Abraham Lincoln was a more fully evolved human than Attila the Hun. Our task as humans is one we "retire from" at risk of our souls. Not hell. Boredom. Loss of meaning.

Staying Young

*Truly I tell you, unless you change and become like
children, you will never enter the kingdom of heaven.*
—Matthew 18:3

Some otherwise insightful people try to hang onto their childhood by going to tanning salons, botoxing their crows' feet, jog-
ging, dyeing, transplanting, outwitting God. Again, the contest
between surfaces and substance. But the urge is real—and God
given, I think. It's just the way such illusionists misimagine the
goal—not to *look* young but to *be* young. To lie down with the
lamb while retaining the leonine ferocity our years have merited.
Paradox time again: both shrewd and receptive, cautious but still
willing to risk (which defines faith).

Many of us also lose the child's curiosity about reasons and
causes: "but *why*?" We teachers and parents need reminding (even
from our own children) "why" is the question that keeps us human. We're the only species blessed/cursed with it, born to ask it,
and keep asking. We were meant to ask odd questions, be discontent with "that's the way it is," cross-examine what "everybody
says." Unless we do, we become no better than sheep or, worse,
robots.

Curiosity costs. But to lose it—for a less-bothered life—is dehumanizing. The death wish.

The teenagers I've spent my life cajoling out of the nest are
smothered by "helicopter parents" whose profoundest wish is to
keep their children from any harm, which deftly swerves them
away from any chance of becoming adult human beings. And the
necessity of risking loss—as we'll see more fully in Chapter 19—
has been the unfailing pattern of every life since the start: birth,
weaning, play, schooling, adolescence, marriage, parenthood, aging. And the struggle continues: God forever discontent with stasis, prolonged stagnation, ungrowth. When God invited humans
beyond other animals, he shrewdly left the beast in us—inertia
and self-involvement—as a daily challenge to keep us reaching.
But God was clever about it! He also plugged in that discontent
that can never be satisfied except by a connection into divinity.

No sane human has failed to feel it. It's just so many try to placate discontent with "junk food" that fizzles too fast.

If you sink into the quicksand again, it's your own fault—when there's all kinds of those Tarzan vines hanging right there within your grasp. You can sit in front of the TV waiting for death with iron resignation, or you can charge your batteries reading to someone blind, or grandparenting a kid with no hope of happiness, or spelling someone caring for a bedridden loved one, or sitting in a retirement home sharing gossip and "editorialized" tales of how we all were once denizens of Olympus, heroes and heroines who struggled through Hades, found ways to lead our men out of their labyrinths, fought on the ringing plains of Troy, shouldered boulders up sky-high mountains even though they always rolled back down, and wrestled with God himself. (Little kids are also willing to suspend disbelief and listen—as long as you yourself really enjoy the lies.) You could also relive the lively times of your life on the social media, like old folks gossiping in rockers on the front porch. It works against arthritis in the fingers rather than in the jaws.

Ever notice a lot of Wikipedia entries offer invitations to edit? If you're over fifty, there's got to be some subject you know more about than some high school kid. There also has to be some teacher at the nearest middle school who wouldn't mind a retired lawyer or engineer or cop or carpenter (or even a retired teacher!) coming around once a month to share seat-of-the-pants experiences available in no textbook. Why not write a book called *How to Stay Sane to the Very End*? It could be a lot of fun even just writing a paragraph here or there. The point isn't publication but liberation. Spend at least fifteen minutes a day using your imagination to dream up ways to surprise somebody that make their faces erupt in a smile. Start with the easy ones, but keep upping the ante on yourself. When you feel ready, go for somebody who looks like they've spent the day sucking those alum styptic pencils shavers use to cauterize nicks.

As I age, much as I'm still addicted to teaching and writing, every morning when the alarm offers the first disequilibrium of the day, I find that more and more I hit the snooze button and curl into that warm pocket in the bedclothes. The womb. Thanatos.

But when I throw off the comfort and get my juices pumping, I feel alive. Which is the other direction from death.

Like confidence, curiosity requires vulnerability. Vulnerability to the truth, wherever the puzzlement might lead; vulnerability to other people, no matter how initially repellent; and vulnerability to the quest to leaving behind something comfortable in order to risk something better. But as Alistair Reed wrote, "Dying is what the living do, Dying is what the loving do."

Specifically human life begins to die when we stop asking, "Why?" Check the subway.

17.

Enchantment

Be thankful for what you have; you'll end up having more. If you concentrate on what you don't have, you'll never, ever have enough.
—Oprah Winfrey

At our age, once you acquiesce to two facts, you discover an invitation to a bigger life, locked right in the jaws of a dilemma. First, you make peace with the inevitability of slowing down and dying, sooner now, rather than later. Everything meaningful in life you have on diminishing borrowed time. That's a natural resource dribbling away day by day, and there's no gauge to tell when "empty" is close. Second, you really should keep recalling you never did anything to be here in the first place. That, too, ought to intensify your appreciation of everything's value—a value that only those of us who've been lucky to last can fully appreciate.

Those ignorable but inexorable facts can instead leech out all the zest in your living, till there's nothing left but iron resignation. You've seen it. However, resilient folks can grab hold of them—like the two contrary poles of a magnet: life and death—and rediscover a whole new force: the indomitable human spirit that transcends both life and death. With a bit of resolve, we can become like children again. Clear-headed people can find the magic is still there, the brightness inside the unpromising. The magic! Provided you don't get distracted by surface stuff like cellulite, wrinkles, paunches, and bunions. The essential—the soul—is always invisible. Unlike the surfaces, you do have final control of that *penetrating* viewpoint.

It's very simple. As you grow, you learn more. If you stayed at twenty-two, you'd always be as ignorant as you were at twenty-two. Aging isn't just decay, you know. It's growth. It's more than the negative that you're going to die, it's also the positive that you understand you're going to die, and that you live a better life because of it.

—Mitch Albom

Because I've really wrapped my head around the gratuitous gift of life and inevitability of death, I never wake up grouchy the way a lot of people do: "Oh, God, *another* day!" Nope. It's "Oh, *God!* Another *day!*" When you realize every day's a gift you did nothing to deserve, it tends to make an honorable person grateful. And vigilant. Forget death catching me with some unspeakable sin on my soul. God forbid death should catch me bored! Or bitter. Or living half-assedly.

Again, it's all in the attitude. If you go out in the morning with your SOB filters on, it's amazing how many SOBs there are in the world. But if you clip on your Jesus glasses—the ones that penetrate the trivial surfaces—you become astonished at the real souls emerging from underneath, the true selves who fear the same things as you do and yearn for the same things as you do: to be found, to be understood, maybe even loved.

> The world is fairly studded and strewn with pennies cast broadside by a generous hand. But—and this is the point—who gets excited by a mere penny? But if you cultivate a healthy poverty and simplicity, so that finding a penny will literally make your day, then, since the world is in fact planted in pennies, you have with your poverty bought a lifetime of days.
>
> —Annie Dillard

In the same way, now that I have a longer perspective on what life means, I can look back at the biggest setbacks I've had—the humiliating mediocre grades, the condescension, the agonies, the lost jobs—and I find that sour old Nietzsche was right. Not a single one didn't make me stronger. They forged a deep leaden keel that let me weather storms that would founder flat-bottoms. Over the course of my unpredictable pilgrimage, I discovered also how shallow my ideas had been, about love, sex, death, success, character, acceptance: meaning. I'm happier to have time to treasure how lucky I've been in being forced to find a reason to keep going. It's how God and I became friends. Before, we were just acquaintances.

For a long while, I puzzled over the ruby slippers in *The Wizard of Oz,* an archetype of leaving our first childhood. When Dorothy's house lands on the Wicked Witch of the East and Glinda the Good Witch shows up, the slippers magically transfer from the dead witch's feet to Dorothy's. So, she's *got* her transport back to Kansas already, yes? Why doesn't Glinda tell her right then, "Just click your heels three times, honey, and say 'There's no place like home'"?

Well, for one thing, there'd be no story, would there? Which, of course, is the point. Dorothy isn't ready to move into the next stage of her life till she's discovered—not proven—that she already *does* have the virtues her three pals seem to lack: courage, intelligence, and love. It's a "test" not from some sadistic teacher to ratify her worthiness, but to prove to *herself* she's ready to take on life in a new way. It's only by rising to new challenges that we lose our fears of inadequacy. We find our right to confidence by *acting* confident. "Fake it till you feel it!"

Then, when she's risen to her challenges, Dorothy can be let in on the secret: all along, the magic in the slippers has been *Dorothy.*

Now, in The Third Age, *we've* set a new, parallel call: to *rediscover* after a lifetime of challenges that old magic that stands in our own shoes.

Like Dorothy moving into the whole new country of adulthood—whose task is to share the newfound self in an entirely new way, our natural deceleration invites us into pulling together all the disparate elements and events of our lives and their particular insights, reforging them into a newly owned, unique personal *wisdom.* Think of all the parables Jesus told about the master who goes off on a trip and, when he returns, asks his faithful servants for a tally of what they've made of his trust. Once again, the greatest monument to your having lived is you.

But now, any wantwit our age should realize we no longer need to "earn our spurs." We've each battled our share of witches and winged monkeys, fire, poisonous poppies, ogrish apple trees. "I'm still *here!*" There's still a whole lot of magic left in our ruby running shoes! Shame to waste it.

What does "wisdom" mean? I have a hunch it consists precisely in having discovered the brightness—the enchantment—inside everything we've encountered all our lives—dotty Dumbledores and duplicitous dragons. As Ignatius Loyola said, "Finding God in all things." We're to extract all the contagious goodness inside the unpromising—and even the detestable. Then to "process" that, like bread fungus that becomes penicillin, distilling a "good infection" to spread everywhere we go: making joy contagious. (That doesn't sound naive, does it?)

What will make us, at least "in the going," fulfilled? I suspect it's contentment to keep asking questions—without hankering for definitive, final answers, grateful we'll never run out of *terras incognitas* to explore. And I suspect success is also rooted in confident serenity to be attentively aware of clues in the faces of everyone around us, as *alert* as a new mother to signals from her newborn child. That watchfulness—continual sensitizing of the mind and heart—is demanding, often without rewards, often fatiguing. But it sure beats dying before you die.

This is the time to be sure that life isn't just "something I went through" or "something that happened *to* me." Rather, I broke through the surfaces under which God was hiding all along. I found the romance inside the commonplace, the gold in Rumpelstiltskin's straw, the enchanted princesses and princes inside all the scullery girls and froggy boys, and within myself I found an adopted peer of the realm of Christ. (Naive?)

The enchanted essential, the Spirit, is invisible, making itself known only in its effects—like the oak within the acorn, like Beethoven inside his embryo, like the spark of God within your own soul. The years assuredly swerved our understandings of those virtues from what they were when we were Dorothy's age. At least they ought to have.

They're worth allowing Paul to enumerate them again: "love, joy, peace, patience, kindness, decency, faithfulness, gentleness and self-control."

Love (*agape, caritas*) has little to do with heart palpitations and is far distant from the need for love that ate at us when we first pulled away from the unquestionable assurance of family. It's caring that defies any challenge. It sums up all the other virtues. True love is at the opposite end of the spectrum from the slavery of teenage infatuations. It's a blank check we hold out that says, "Take advantage of this at any time, no matter how inconvenient." We make that offer even to God. It took us years to learn that. Ma Joad in *The Grapes of Wrath*.

Joy (*chara, gaudium*) shows itself most definitely and paradoxically in hard times. Joy can't be sought in itself but arises only as a byproduct of other endeavors. It's the legitimate pride that comes from saying, "By God, I did my best today." It blossoms automatically in a soul headed in the right direction, a grateful "victim" of God's grace. Robin Williams in *Dead Poets' Society*, when he's fired and his boys jump off their desks saying, "Captain, my Captain."

Peace (*eirene, pax*) is the serenity that comes from "having it all together, wholeness." Surely not the "peace the world gives," the ads for Caribbean vacations. Rather, the easefulness of the tightrope walker, those who defuse bombs, terminal ward nurses. Not lack of challenges but confidence standing up to them. We've all been there before. The two Australian soldiers in *Breaker Morant*, joining hands to face the firing squad.

Patience (*makrothumia, longanimitas*) comes from having a reason to endure, to keep going. What Frankl shows in *Man's Search for Meaning*: a profound sense of purpose—an anchor in a truth outside oneself that gives substance to the resolve that "I will *not* quit." Thomas More in *A Man for All Seasons*.

Kindness (*chrestotes, benignitas*) is the will to act for the good even of those who tax your patience, even when they find your caring cruel. Like all these virtues, it's honestly selfless, with no hope of a return. Giving is its own recompense. Judd Hirsch, Conrad's psychiatrist in *Ordinary People*.

Decency (*agathosune, bonitas*) is often rendered "goodness," which is unhelpfully vague. "Decency" seems to specify it a bit more: doing what is "fitting, right, just." Maybe the best word is "dependable." Gary Cooper in *High Noon*.

Faithfulness (*pistis, fides*) means "dependable," but it adds the dimension of "watchfulness, attentiveness," the vigilance that goes well beyond "being there for them." It's the alertness of a mother when her infant breathes funny. Sam Gangee in *The Lord of the Rings*.

Modesty (*prautes, modestia*): "unpretentious" is more fitting than "meekness," which has prissy connotations. Little to do with avoiding brash clothing choices; less concerned with curbing sexual temptations than with negating narcissism. Melanie Wilkes in *Gone with the Wind*.

Self-control (*egkrateia, continentia*) accepts responsibility for whatever one does. It has little to do with the whip and chair of the animal tamer we recall so well from our childhood as it does to an honest, adult awareness—and acceptance—not only of one's weaknesses but of one's strengths. Gregory Peck in *To Kill a Mockingbird*.

I hope you note that none of these virtues can be "captured" in a catechism. We who claim to live the Christian life *are* the lessons—the way we "carry ourselves."

As St. Francis of Assisi said, "Preach the gospel always. If necessary, use words."

18.
Choosing the Inescapable

He not busy being born is busy dying.
—Bob Dylan

Carl Jung wrote that "neurosis is always a substitute for legitimate suffering." It's usually far more painful trying to weasel around unacceptable truths than to face them, flat on. Hamlet's a prime example. And a great passel of Hebrew prophets tried to elude the call: Moses stammering his inability, Jeremiah pleading his youth, and Jonah hightailing it diametrically away from that wicked old Nineveh toward Spain. Isaiah and Simon Peter beg God to leave them alone, because they're sinful, unworthy. Not really. Just infatuated with inertia.

When we edge toward the evening of our lives, after a full lifetime of "days' work," it's ever so tempting to pull off to the roadside and enjoy the view. Leave all the fuss and challenges to folks who still have the stamina—and idealism—to be intrigued simply by a challenge. Trouble is, stasis isn't quite what God had in mind for everything else. Nothing in the universe I can think of fulfills its purpose by just "being there." Even brainless planets are attracting and repelling one another every minute. And they've been at it quite a bit longer than I have. Something specifically human bristles at being as negligible as an appendix. Milton wrote, "They also serve who only stand and wait." But with all this "rebirth" business connected with God, I've come to believe that the God Jesus called "the God of the living, not of the dead" (Matthew 22:32) rightfully expects that some people will *really* notice when I'm *genuinely* dead, not still in a walking coma.

My hunch is the "God of the living"—the God whose only question at the final reckoning will be about our self-forgetful kindness—rejects zombies, "the living dead," who drag through each day with granite submission, giving others the heebie-jeebies with guilt for being alive and happy. The challenge the aging are called to surmount is ways to alchemize inertia.

Which is more seductive to you personally: Playing golf or bridge or playing with broken children? Shopping or teaching English as a second language? Fishing or filling trays in a half-way house? Reading to the blind? Listening at a hotline? Anything beats being nobly lonely. Is there ever a moratorium on our inner urge to feel useful? Which requires being used.

The great Reinhold Niebuhr wrote what might be the best prayer since the Our Father ("thy will be done") to offer liberation from the itch clever people always have to artfully dodge the will of God: "God, grant me the serenity to accept the things I cannot change, the courage to change the things I can, and the wisdom to know the difference."

Change—especially at an age when we feel beyond the need of more surprises—is always a kind of suffering, at least in its broadest sense of losing something one's comfortable with, at the risk of finding something better. It's the root of all stories. The Chinese curse captures it: "May you live in interesting times." Meaning, may you have fascinating stories to tell, cluttered with captivating dragons, whiskered witches, and storm-swept cliffs.

More than that, suffering is really *necessary*. Would anyone truly value warm, sunny days who'd never know cold rainy days? Or light without having been afraid of the dark? Don't the people we love show their true value when we realize we have them only on borrowed time? An honest awareness of suffering cuts through the fakery of all the commercials and sitcoms.

Some things simply can't be changed: her husband isn't coming back, you have in fact been fired, this cancer is inoperable. Struggle to change the inescapable will drive you crazy. The difference between optimism and hope is vast. Optimism chortles, "The sun'll come out tomorrow!" in the face of the most expert meteorologists. Hope is the refusal to quit—even though the outcome is foregone and all is lost—except my soul. Those who survived the Nazi camps know the difference. So did Sisyphus: "I will *not* quit!"

Some things can be changed—with discipline, drive, determination, and pride. "I wish I weren't so moody. Why does my friend keep avoiding me? I will *never* forgive that woman! There's nothing good on TV!"

The wisdom part of the prayer at least ought to come with age. But experience is *not* "the best teacher." Only experience *reflected* on, digested, transformed into understanding. Distilling out the truth, the magic, not just adults from teenagers but from all other animals. If we choose to use it.

No need that your story has to become dull as dishwater just because you've lain down your sword and shield. Even after ten years agony in Troy and ten years more on the seas, Tennyson's *Ulysses* was still infected with the itch only humans are born with:

Tho' much is taken, much abides; and tho'
We are not now that strength which in old days
Moved earth and heaven, that which we are, we are;
One equal temper of heroic hearts,
Made weak by time and fate, but strong in will
To strive, to seek, to find, and not to yield.

That itch to search for experiences that can lead to deeper meaning isn't as devil-may-care for us oldsters as it used to be. The cost of it has become ever clearer. And yet, "Just to sit and be makes a no one of me." Every change and every threat of it is an unwelcome opportunity. Call it grace. It's a new call—when Dorothy and Frodo and Luke Skywalker and Leia are longer in the tooth and creakier in the joints—but it's still seductive to the residual aliveness deep down in us. A lure to discover a fresher perspective, a more life-giving attitude. That seems, for anyone open to the truth, the persistent, undeniable will of God: death and resurrection.

God is discontent with once and for all. As Chesterton wrote, God (who, unlike us, has never aged) is like a little child who keeps saying, "Do it again! Do it again!" To the planets, to the seasons, to lovers, to each of our souls: "Conceive Christ in you again. Today! Even better this time!" Since the Big Bang, our Creator has shown an inexorable preference for change over stasis. All over the universe, stars are busy dying so that they can emerge into something better. Cosmology and evolution show that making something out of nothing just once is hardly enough for this insatiable Creator.

The Spirit of God we invoke so incautiously isn't a dove; she's a spitfire Spirit: a tigress. She brooded over the waters of chaos at the beginning and demanded it line up as cosmos. This Spirit electrified life in inanimate matter, then feeling in animals, then the relentless search for meaning and purpose in human beings. This Spirit quickened the Son of God and wrapped him in the web of a hillbilly girl's womb. This Spirit animated Jesus when he cleared the Temple with nothing but a handful of rope and rage. In her, the lioness lies down with the ewe—but without losing her leonine ferocity. Jesus underscored that vital energy: "I came that they may have life, and have it abundantly" (John 10:10). No "use by" date. Of his Father, he said, "He is God not of the dead but of the living" (Matthew 22:32). It's being still energized by that kind of being alive that lets us bypass purgatory, where that's the principal lesson.

What we "celebrate" in such an uncomprehending way each Christmas ought to be a staggering fulfillment of God's intolerance of success as "arriving" rather than change, *striving*. In fact, the incarnation could well be the very *reason* for creation, what all cosmology and evolution have been all about all along. Everything they were pointing toward: from inert matter to growth, to sensation and intuition, to rational thought, and now into the ultimate exhilaration of the soul—insertion into the aliveness of God.

Christmas celebrates that the Creator of all universes, the imaginer of the periodic table, the energizer of the beyond-cosmic thrill of life itself, the progenitor of thought, the original crucible of love has *become* flesh—one of us. The utterly unchangeable has yielded himself up to change. In order to show us how to do it well. With dignity.

The Holy One whom Isaiah and Handel call "Wonderful Counselor! The Mighty God! The Everlasting Father! The Prince of Peace"—this unutterably holy personage compacted himself and his power and his love into the most fragile being we know: a human infant. It's no longer unthinkable—or undignified (as Deists insist)—that Almighty God needed someone else to change his diapers, that he had to learn how to learn—just as all humans must, that he would put up with pettiness, small-mindedness, catty neighbors, that he would finally come face to face with hatred, misunderstanding, revilement, betrayal, desertion, flesh flogged to the bone, a death so degrading it was reserved for society's most detestable. All that is rooted in that holy night we've made Hallmark sweet instead of overwhelming.

Like the unlikelihood of the universe from that tiny singularity, the oak from the acorn, the power of all poetry and music and science from an infinitesimal zygote, Almighty God has joined with us in weakness, vulnerability, uncertainty, and suffering—to show us how it's done. To show us what he intended human beings to be from before the start.

It's frightening to think of that kind of willing degradation. Astounding to comprehend the God who is beyond limit constricting himself. And to make himself even more accessible to us, he does it day after day, in the Eucharist: "He comes, stilly as rain, into the darkness of our bellies—God in a bit of bread, to bring morning into our souls!"

Even nonbelievers see that pattern of new life emerging from the taken for granted. It's been the life lesson all along. Every life disruption Erik Erikson calls a "crisis of disequilibrium," a lesson plan built right into the *process* of human maturing. The first radical change is birth itself. For nine months you were closer to paradise than you'll ever again be on earth: warm, floating, fed, without a care simply because you couldn't think. Then suddenly, through no fault of your own, you're thrust out into the cold and noise. But without it, you would have died. That first lesson forces the child's body along the first steps to physical independence. And all the succeeding crises invite the same: a profounder way of being alive.

After a year or so, when children naturally develop muscle control, parents have to start imposing limits—what Freudians call a superego—dos and don'ts the child can't fathom but keep infants from pulling lamps down on their heads, and they impose bottle and potty training. The lesson again calls the child to amplify his or her freedom from dependence. Whoever fails at that—or is shielded from that—could well come back and seek the same unhealthy support later from chemicals or sex or power. Parents then impose another separation: booted out in the cold to play with the other willful children, freeing them to settle differences without adult intrusions. Then they're deserted in the kindergarten doorway, to learn the skills of the tribe, industry, competence to support themselves. Then the atomic intrusion: adolescence—a time of utter bewilderment, the call to discover and have confidence in a personally validated self. Yet again, in the ideal plan, one then takes that self-possession and freely offers it to another in intimacy and partnership, slowly learning the difference between romance and genuine love. Which leads for most in that natural order to the generativity of adulthood: parenthood, yet again stretching open the latitude of one's attention, concern, self-giving: one's soul self.

And here we are, at the final stage. But to treat this time of our lives as "retirement" from more than a job would be the slow death of the soul. Treading water, surviving vs. being alive.

Do you see the hard outline of a "personality trait" in the God who gave us life for a *purpose?* There's nowhere we can turn that it doesn't manifest itself: death and rebirth. The only way to flee it is into neurosis.

Aging is a brand-new invitation to ask ourselves how convincingly we're still saying, "Thy will be done," after all these years. God's will—as all those prophets discovered—can be evaded only so long. Sooner or later, just because of who God is and who we are, trying to escape God's will—the truth—keeps getting more and more frustrating. The only way to find peace is to *choose* to accept the inescapable. Look at two we at least claim as models of humanity, Our Lady and Our Lord. Look at the annunciation and the agony in the garden: "Not my will but your will be done" (Luke 1:38; 22:42).

> I fled Him down the nights and down the days
> I fled Him down the arches of the years
> I fled Him down the labyrinthine ways
> Of my own mind, and in the midst of tears
> I hid from him, and under running laughter.

Up vistaed hopes I sped and shot precipitated
Adown titanic glooms of chasmed fears
From those strong feet that followed, followed after.
— Francis Thompson

Think of poor runaway Jonah, in the belly of his great fish, sloshing around in clots of kelp and half-digested sea bass, being returned by the persistent Yahweh to his destiny in Nineveh.

We'll encounter God everywhere we turn—thrumming under the surfaces of everything we touch, lurking around every corner, We'll encounter him every step of the way—even in the dragons, and demons of hellfire, and sullen sales clerks. The unexpected is God in disguise.

Christ and the Blessed Mother are so smothered in doctrines trying to box in their incomprehensible goodness that, even though I've gratefully shed most of what I was taught about them in theology, those years still—to my shame—give them an aloofness they surely didn't project when they sweated at work and lay gratefully to sleep at night. But someone who, at least for me, enfleshes the "serenity . . . courage . . . and wisdom" of the Niebuhr prayer is St. Joseph. There's nothing at all dramatic about him. He's just a truly decent human being, as are we.

The whole cluster of my notions of St. Joseph are tangled up with all my memories of my dad. The reason is that they at least *seemed* so much alike. Nazareth was a hillbilly town ("Can anything good come from Nazareth?"), and my dad came from Walkerton, Ontario, which is about as nowhere as you can get. The gospel gussies up Joseph's credentials with genealogies of famous forebears, which are drained of all power for us today. And the first time Dad got his name in the paper was his obituary. Joseph was a handyman, and Dad drove a truck serving mom-and-pop food stores. They were quiet men, undemonstrative, religious, unpretentious, dutiful. And as with Mary and Joseph, my mom—through no fault of her own—brought out the greatness in Dad. She was in the hospital at least once a year for more than twenty years. And Dad never complained. Never. And, God, how he *worked*. Dawn to dusk, every day but the Sabbath. After breakfast Sunday morning, he'd fall asleep reading the paper. There are two words that capture for me the inner balance and solidity of Dad and Joseph: "steady" and "ready." For me, those words are synonyms for "holy."

No matter what mind-boggling surprise broke out, they said, "All right. I'm here." Joseph found his innocent wife was pregnant, and she gave him the most egregious explanation. Mom was just out of danger after a heart attack when she tumbled down the stairs and broke her arm, or leg, or both. Serenity never seemed to have any lasting power. But at every unwelcome challenge, they stood up to it. Dependably. No bitterness. No compromises. Everything that "faithful" means. "If you need me to, I will."

The secret to coping with unexpected, unwelcome change nestles in the old cliché: "When life gives you lemons, make lemonade." Which takes imagination. And resilience. The life wish.

Because that's what God has always been: The alchemist. God takes the unpromising and vivifies it. Nothing transforms into everything. Dead matter "learns" to grow. Life metamorphoses into "being alive"—feeling, sensing, moving. Not enough. Let's make a creature who can talk back, throw us curves, keep challenging. Still not enough. Let's send our son down and show him how to do it right.

The message of the divine incarnation is forgiveness and resurrection. Or perhaps even into a single word: *transfiguration*. Think of that wonderful final verse from "The Battle Hymn of the Republic":

> In the beauty of the lilies
> Christ was born across the sea,
> With a glory in his bosom
> that transfigures you and me;
> As he died to make men holy,
> let us die to make men free,
> while God is marching on.

When Jesus was transfigured before Peter, James, and John (Matthew 17), his godliness burned through his flesh, blazing. That's the human task: to find the God light within ourselves and then let it *shine*! "Let your light shine before others, so that they may see your good works and give glory to your Father in heaven" (Matthew 5:16).

Cats, they say, have nine lives, which means they get nine times more exhilaration out of living than we do. There's a cost, though. In order to have nine lives, you have to die nine times, each time with no less pain. "Unless the grain of wheat falls to the earth and dies, it remains just a grain of wheat. But if it dies, it produces much fruit" (John 12:24).

> This little light of mine
> I'm going to let it shine
> Let it shine, let it shine, let it shine!

My soul magnifies the Lord. When we come alive, we *are* the greater glory of God.

Sure beats brooding.

Only doubt—being off balance, in a disequilibrium—can release the God-given urge within us passed onto us from the same divine force who's smitten with evolution and resurrection, starting over again—better this time.

One time I asked a very wise nun, "How do you get all the answers from your head down into your guts where all the confusion is?" Without missing a beat she said, "Hm. Go stare at a tree. Or a flower." What? What kind of answers can you get doin' that? But there was such an easy serenity in her face, I had to confess she knew something—accepts something, yields to something—that I really had to rediscover. To be humble of heart.

Getting older is definitely not just a job, but a mission. A wonderful story shows the difference. Long ago, a traveler came upon a site in London where swarms of workers were building a grand church. He saw men digging a ditch and asked what exactly they were doing. The first replied, "Hey! I'm doing what I'm told. I want to make a living for my kids." The second replied, "Me? I'm digging a ditch from here to that stake over there." But the third leaned on his shovel and, with a gleam in his eye, said, "Me? I'm helping Christopher Wren build this bloody great *cathedral*!"

19.
Faith Means Confidence

There is no fear in love, but perfect love casts out
fear; for fear has to do with punishment.
—1 John 4:18

Anyone who claims faith but lacks confidence is self-delusive. The root of confidence—not just the word, but the reality—*is* faith (*fides*). How can anyone claim real faith in the gospel and remain timid when the One who calls and sends is Jesus who worked miracles with mud and spit?

> The Lord appointed seventy others and sent them on ahead of him in pairs to every town and place where he himself intended to go. "Cure the sick.... I've given you authority to tread on snakes and scorpions, and over all the power of the enemy; and nothing will hurt you."
>
> (Luke 10)

Notice Jesus gives this commission to *seventy* people—no mention of sex, theological training, or ordination. No hint they might have cooked and served the Last Supper. Yet Jesus empowers "ordinary layfolk" with the exact *same* goals and abilities he gave The Twelve—powers Catholics have long restricted to clergy and hierarchy, only to those specially trained and officially ordained. Jesus summoned his twelve disciples and gave them authority over unclean spirits, to cast them out, and to cure every disease and every sickness (Matthew 10:1).

Admittedly, in neither commissioning is there mention of sacramental or administrative power. But as Jesus' description of the final judgment testifies (Matthew 23), the only skill needed for the ordinary, day-to-day Christian mission is a kind heart, and the only authority is the confidence in having been called and the power to see Christ in the needy. The power and mission come not from training or ordination but from accepting the call and all it entails—as adults.

Nor should we get sidetracked into literalism—reading the Christian mission with materialist eyes, as if the only real demons were horned devils and the only genuine snakes literal vermin—any more than we should read the "harvest" as literally wielding sickles in a wheat field. We encounter demons of self-doubt and barren childhoods. Constant failure and bitter marriages are agonizing diseases, as are alcoholism, loneliness, metastasizing debt. Serpents of greed and self-indulgence ooze from our TV sets. It needs neither training nor ordination to recognize and exorcise them from our children. It takes love, trust in God and in ourselves, and a critical mind.

Most people our age today were taught to be lifelong children, "seen, not heard." The subliminal message, all those years: "pay, pray, and obey."

I risk overkill flogging truly good people who trained those of us who can recall Pius XII, who (unreflectively) lament the "good old Baltimore Catechism" that nailed down all answers with certainty. We were like recruits in boot camp with no need to decide anything: when to rise, salute, turn left, sleep, die. Anything not forbidden was compulsory, anything not compulsory was forbidden. Dehumanizing, since it rendered God-given freedom meaningless.

Freedom, by its very nature, has to be unencumbered by just such compulsion and threats as the law imposed. God invites autonomy (which he offers no other species)—*not* to obey, *not* to love him in return. His reason for that incautious generosity seems rooted in his desire for a species to love freely, unforced by the hard-wired obedience of all other species.

Obedience compelled by fear of hell or hope of heaven isn't what Jesus was after. Such a pledge of faith is no more genuine than a shotgun wedding.

But freedom is tricky, like giving a loaded revolver to a chimp. Intelligence lets us see how hurtful freedom can be. Dostoevsky's Grand Inquisitor said, "Man is tormented by no greater anxiety than to find someone quickly to whom he can hand over that great gift of freedom with which the ill-fated creature is born." The reason's obvious: to be genuinely free, one needs to know all the options, and independence from narcissism to choose even the more costly option if it's the best. Genuine freedom requires the individual to *think*. But Bertrand Russell said, "Many would rather die than think. Most do." Check school dropout rates. Opinion polls. Congress.

As a result, under the guise of self-sacrificial benevolence, the Grand Inquisitor proposes the church remove from ordinary wretches the need to think and sets up a vast matrix of dogmas, laws, decrees—with this-world and next-world sanctions for challenging them. Very simply, "Do exactly what we tell you to, and you'll be as happy as you could ever hope to be, now and forever." The price of security is an enslaved conscience.

Dostoevsky's assertion about the need for the more enlightened to "rectify human frailty" ("save the poor bastards from themselves") is not exclusively a critique against organized religion. That accusation could as well point at Karl Marx or Hitler. In fact, Richard Dawkins and Christopher Hitchens are more dogmatic and apostolic in their crusade to liberate believers than any pope was to dissenters. Any ad agency is evangelical in its crusade to liberate the benighted from congenital inadequacy (and cash). We owe it to our young to exorcize those demons.

The Baltimore Catechism was just such mind-warping propaganda. So, I suggest, is the new *Catechism of the Catholic Church*. They preclude any need to think. Or, in fact, any need to have faith, except in those experts who wrote it. They bar any intrusion of humanity into our creaturely servitude. But love isn't love if it's stimulus/response.

Orthodoxy, clearly, was not the original Christian plan and focus.

The Sermon on the Mount

Many our age still read the Beatitudes with the same childish eyes and minds they originally brought to those stunning paradoxes—before we were capable of sensing or handling paradox. "People living in squalor are lucky because God loves the poor more than he loves us. . . . The unhappier you are, the happier

God is. . . . God delights in boys and girls (old ladies and gentlemen) who are meek, know their place, don't act up or complain. . . . Blessed are those who show a stiff upper lip to injustice and bear it in noble silence. . . . Blessed are the merciful, but don't look for too much of that in schools, business, or wars, where tough skin is unavoidable and necessary. . . . Blessed are the pure in heart, which means avoiding sexual temptations [which at our age are now happily out of reach]. . . . Blessed are peacemakers [if one remembers 'national security' and 'the good of the whole Church,' which often preempt personal conscience if it becomes arrogant]."

Best leave the final two Beatitudes unquoted. They defy the irenic mind-set we want in our children and hope (against all reason) to achieve in our waning years. "Blessed are the persecuted" simply will not "compute" to either the potential recruits or veterans. Our lifelong purpose as parents has been to "give them the best we can" and *shield* them from precisely the disturbances the early Christians faced. Some of us have protected them even from negative feelings arising from an inferior grade in school.

The final beatitude is insupportable: "Blessed are you when people revile you and persecute you and utter evil against you falsely on my account." Such sentiments might have been pertinent in early Christian persecutions. Or the Reformation. Or the French Revolution. Maybe even in the early twentieth century when Catholics faced entrenched Protestantism, Masonry, godless communism. But we do the church no good by appearing to be discontents and quacks.

The unforeseen result of our American assimilation, of course, is our dilution as Catholics. In escaping what we accepted as kids, that "Catholics are number one," being R.C. is no longer seriously significant. Check out a wedding. The videos and reception outclass the Mass by light years. The photographer beats out the priest. One more triumph of superficiality over substance. Other than opposing abortion and birth control, what (in God's name) do we stand *for*?

Good question. These pages are an attempt to seduce you to

go looking for the answer. Your own. Hints are scattered throughout. But don't expect me to serve them up. In a schema. Like a catechism.

As the human invitation (morality) tempts us to rise above all other species, the Christian invitation invites us *beyond* human uprightness and decency into the way of living Jesus demonstrated by his living/dying/coming back for more. And the way he lived and dealt with life—beyond "being moral"—should be clear by now. Don't suffer life. Wrestle with it.

Nor does he hint that, after you've struggled with that for a lifetime, you have the option to "retire." Formed Christians ought to be intimidating.

—"You are the salt of the earth, but if the salt loses it taste. . . ."

—"You are the light of the world. . . . [You] cannot be hid."

—"Unless your righteousness exceeds that of [the Catechisms and rule books] you will never enter the kingdom of heaven."

—"Don't worry about world-class sins like murder; guard against petty sins like anger, calling anybody 'loser,' going to worship with a grudge festering in your soul. Maybe you're safe from full-out adultery, but do you 'use sex' to sell things, to restrict others' lives?"

—Here's some you *couldn't* worry about as kids: "Give to anyone who begs from you—even illegal foreigners. Don't refuse anyone a loan when you can afford it. And stop worrying about what you're going to eat tomorrow. Stop fussing about what you wear."

And we're sent to heal. The heartsick, the bereaved, the overwhelmed. It can be as simple as, "Let's have lunch." Often, the only thing close to healing is wrapping your arms around them and whispering, "You're not alone, you know." So many people feel alone, when they're not. But often we're too polite, too falsely humble to breech their defenses and offer ourselves.

We've been told so many times we no longer question it that the Creed we say every Sunday is the core of Christian belief, and it is the Trinity, the incarnation, the suffering/death/resurrection of Jesus, the dependable Spirit. Those are nonnegotiable doctrines. You can be a saint, like Gandhi or Camus, but if you reject those, you're not Christian. Just as you can't eat meat and call yourself vegetarian. But those are restrictive, definitive, simply *organizational.* They hardly reveal themselves in the way you act, treat other people, prioritize values.

Gandhi himself said, "I like your Christ . . . but your Christians are so unlike your Christ."

The difference is right here: The Creed was forged by theologians. The Beatitudes come right from Christ. No finely incised, masterfully honed, waterproof definitions. He washed their feet. There you have it. Compacted into an action, not words. Only then did he articulate it for the less gifted: "By *this* everyone will know that you are my disciples, if you *show* love for one another." Even for Judas, who was on his way out the door.

Surely by this time, your ideas of what love truly means have grown enormously, far richer and more refined than the first time you ingested those words. Not just what love means, but what it costs.

The core of "Christian" is "Unless you lose yourself—even shyness and shortcomings—you'll never find yourself. Your salt becomes insipid and your soul stales and goes impotent. Your light must disperse itself into the darkness in order to bring the world to life." Eucharist bread has to be *broken* apart before the Spirit of Christ within it can enter and enliven others' spirits. And God is irrepressibly polite. He stands at your door and knocks. He'll never enter uninvited.

Bishop Desmond Tutu opens the possibility of Christian adulthood:

> Now Jesus seems to say to the scribe, "Hey, life is more exhilarating as you try to work out the implications of your faith rather than living by rote, with ready-made second-hand [catechism] answers, fitting an unchanging paradigm to a shifting, changing, perplexing, and yet fascinating world." Our faith, our knowledge that God is in charge, must make us ready to take risks, to

125

be venturesome and innovative; yes, to dare to walk where angels might fear to tread.

Jesus never held anything back, not even anger at Peter, Pharisees, money changers. From saccharine holy pictures that warped our understanding, we got the idea Jesus was *only* "meek and mild," a good little boy who knew his place, minded his manners. That's not the Jesus you find in the gospels. He accused; he challenged; he screamed out on the cross. At the Last Supper, he broke *himself* up and passed around the pieces. At the crucifixion, he gave it all up till he didn't even have any blood left.

In the boardroom (coffee room, teachers' room, conference room), at the poker table, on the playing field, what would happen if you consistently "give yourself away"? That's the soul trapped inside all those rules. Do you really believe that as much as you believe "buy low, sell high" and "beware of strangers" or "do others before they do you"?

The diametric opposite of Christianity is paranoia.

Being Ready (at Last!) for Life

I always imagined as a kid that adults had some kind of inner toolbox full of shiny tools: the saw of discernment, the hammer of wisdom, the sandpaper of patience. But then when I grew up I found that life handed you these rusty bent old tools—friendships, prayer, conscience, honesty—and said "do the best you can with these, they will have to do." And mostly, against all odds, they do.

—Anne Lamott

You've probably noticed that, in every folktale, going all the way back to the caves, the hero or heroine is always pathetically impaired. Not only do they have no confidence but, judging by the world's norms, no slightest reason to be. They're the third child, with detestable siblings and hard-hearted parents, or the young heroine has anesthetizing breath, or the hero sports a head like a warthog (without tusks, but ugly enough to make other kids gag). The obvious reason is that wise storytellers wanted kids in the audience to identify with the beleaguered heroine or hero (since there's never been a kid born, since the beginning, who wasn't gravely misunderstood). And the reason they wanted identification is so kids start to realize that with pluck and luck—and the help of kindly strangers—they'll live happily ever after. Well . . . we hope.

But that was then; this is now. We ourselves are no longer callow novices. After all our adventures (provided they didn't just occur *to* us, wear us down like a waterfall over rock), our new "position" in the never-ending story is to *be* Gandalf, Glinda the Good, Obi-Wan Kenobi, the Fairy Godmother.

Well . . . okay. But . . . uh . . . how?

Jesus says, "Don't prepare a defense in advance" (Luke 21:14), and the Greek word Luke uses is an actor's word, meaning memorize lines and practice gestures. How can you prepare set-speeches for a situation you can't even envision, a game where chance sends rain on your parade, other players rush onstage with monkey wrenches? Some church folk offer you catechisms of perfect answers to every situation. In all honesty, I can't. Instead I teach improvisation skills: *thinking* for yourself. The confidence to step up, step in, and improvise comes from faith, trust, *fides*, in the Spirit within you.

The first step is a seismic shift in viewpoint from when we left behind Christian learning—perspective, a new value matrix, the point of view we've earned from making it to this end of the gauntlet. We have to pull up short and acknowledge that the worst things that ever happened to us in our lives are the greatest *gifts* we ever received (cf. the crucifixes that have dotted our hallways and highways). Our wrinkles and scars are our validation.

Like all those heroines and heroes of folktales and sagas and myths and Bible stories, our challenges have *already* hollowed us out, not into a vacuum, a mere emptiness, but like a womb, a fertile expectancy, ready to be quickened with new life. The true self. Our unique soul. Ready for the final challenge: preparing the future world and future church. Sharing wisdom wrung from wrongs.

But, having heard a great many confessions from truly good

people, I'm convinced most Third Age Catholics are still operating as if they were at the *beginning* of the quest rather than the end, that we're still as clueless and feckless as Dorothy Gale and Jack of Beanstalk fame! And the formal church has done its best to *keep* us there—docile sheep, "my dear children."

Look in the mirror! Do you still look *callow*, untested? Or do you look like Alec Guinness and Maggie Smith? No need to set out on a journey to fill your backpack with lessons. They're already there! Waiting to become profitable for someone young just starting out.

First, take the to time check the arsenal of convictions you've forged over a lifetime—like love being more important than security; so are curiosity, growth, vulnerability. Risking is a lot more fun than security. No matter how dark the skies or how implacable the odds, you now have solid grounds for confidence—*fides*, faith—in yourself. In baseball, winning only one-third of the time is *really* good. You can climb any Calvary, no matter how degrading, with dignity, your own soul cupped in your hands, sure there's resurrection on the other side. That's Christianity in a nutshell: confident humility, unassuming pride. I never saw that in a catechism.

Many snort when I say I once was really shy. But I really was. First one bashed in grade-school dodgeball games. And my grades during the first six god-awful years of philosophy and theology were enough to scuttle any pretensions.

But just before I was ordained, I'd swamped myself in self-hatred, paralyzing my ability to do anything for anyone—even myself. But God suddenly reached down into my quicksand of doubt and grabbed me. Like drowning in light. I *knew*—with no need or power to prove it—that I was in the presence of God. And I was *accepted*. And if God accepted me—wounds and warts and all, not only accepted but approved, who the hell was I to pretend I wasn't? The only person getting in God's way was me. Confidence comes from faith—from conviction, not a catechism.

Maturity in Christ, of course, also entails challenging those responsible when the Sunday homilies are a direct obstacle to your faith.

The Heresy of Human Sheephood

An endless phalanx of well-intentioned religion teachers, homilists, and retreat givers, beginning from my own mother, made me abhor the remotest temptation to be vain. Even legitimately proud. Even, God help us, confident. John Ruskin said, "Pride is at the bottom of all mistakes." Had he been less of an aesthete, he might also have said, "Lack of pride is at the bottom of all mediocre lives."

No hubris in a bemedaled Special Olympics kid's face bursting with a smile, a mother exhausted from labor hearing her baby's first cry, the final marathon runner with his fists on his knees throwing up. That's a universe away from vanity, and anyone who convinces "these little ones" to doubt themselves, belittle themselves, believe they're humble nobodies, "It would be better for him to be thrown into the sea with a millstone tied around his neck" (Luke 17:2).

The parable of the talents is daunting. The seemingly poorly gifted third servant, knowing his master was a hard man, buried his talent. He was prudent, humble, self-demeaning. In a word, a coward. According to the meek and gentle Jesus, what our master will say to the falsely humble: "Throw that worthless servant outside, into the darkness, where there will be weeping and gnashing of teeth."

In a sheepfold, anyone with the courage to stand up and be counted, to say "This is wrong!" to refuse to shut up, will invariably be called "arrogant." They could even, like Jesus, be crucified for refusing to be humble.

Who cares about the opinions of small-minded people? Most of us.

So there we have the challenge of the gospel: Climb to the rooftops and shout the good news that no sin is unforgivable and no life is ultimately lost, that what transpires in the heart transcends all rules, that striving is more meaningful than achieving. To be silent, safe, impotent is self-condemning.

Most of our religious understanding was sown with terror about sexual weaknesses, but nothing about the sheepishness, fearfulness, crippling humility that Jesus says leads to "weeping and gnashing of teeth." And in Revelation, God says, "I wish you were either hot or cold. But because you are lukewarm, I vomit you out of my mouth."

Oh, my.

20.
Tolerance for Ambiguity

To learn which questions are unanswerable, and
not to answer them: this skill is most needful in
times of stress and darkness.
— Ursula K. Le Guin

In *Fiddler on the Roof*, the villagers exuberantly celebrate the joys of tradition: centuries-old customs that always gave meaning to their lives and identity as a separate people. Yet those same traditions dictated that, when Tevye's daughter married a Christian, she must be treated as dead. Tradition insists, against his innermost heart, that he no longer may love his own daughter.

Even nonbelievers need traditions—at least a shallow Christmas they find nowhere else. Traditions give a comfortable shape to our years. But like all other things on the face of the earth—food, wine, sex, law, even love—traditions are good servants, wicked masters. What's more, there are good laws and traditions and bad laws and traditions. Which are which?

St. Paul settled the bickering in Corinth over charismatics disrupting the Eucharist with what they claimed was the Spirit speaking in tongues: let them alone and see. Does this effusion result in their being more loving, caring, and generous outside the church? If so, it's of God. Or does it make them condescending and sneering to those not thus gifted? If so, it's of the evil one. Thanatos.

When Clare Luce was considering conversion to Catholicism she used to look at Catholics and say to herself, "You say you have the truth. Well, the truth should set you free, give you joy. Can I *see* your freedom? Can I *feel* your joy?" Which of our specifically Catholic laws and traditions set us free and bring us joy, and which bring heartbreak and dehumanization?

Granted, the church enjoins certain options that, in nonobjective moments, we find hateful or forbids options we find desirable—yet we know, objectively, they are simply hard truths programmed into the natures of things by a God not answerable to us, like "Thou shalt not kill thy boss." But could there be issues about which the current (even centuries-old) view of the official church is objectively wrong and the informed individual conscience is objectively right?

Scripture

The two touchstones of Catholic orthodoxy are scripture and tradition (and scripture is itself a record of traditions). In the last century, our view of scripture's normative function changed radically from rigid literalist doctrines into a metaphorical guide to understand ourselves as human beings, transformed by the continuing influence of Christ and by our membership in a worshiping, serving community. Commitment became more important than righteousness; saving one's soul from atrophy here and now is a truer goal than saving it from some future hell.

Most Christians are no longer disquieted that the gospels were probably not written by eyewitnesses. They're at peace with them as approximative, yet trustworthy as a modern biography reconstructing honestly the life and message of a person fifty years dead. Literate adult Christians aren't too troubled that stories of the Magi, Peter walking on water, or the Ascension may not be literally, historically true—yet they do tell, symbolically, life-giving truths: Jesus came not only for poor, unschooled Jewish peasants but for wealthy, learned gentiles as well; if we keep our eyes only on Jesus, not on our own limitations, we can do what we thought impossible; Jesus went into another dimension of existence that antedated the four dimensions we're able to perceive, a dimension in which we, too, exist here and now. *Not accurate and yet meaningful.*

Does it "ring true"—whether reported by St. Peter, or Augustine, or a modern theologian, or a bishop, or my own mother?

In our early training, scripture was poetry analyzed by accountants, forgetting it was written by people trying to physicalize realities that are true but not physical—what William James described with admirable lack of specificity: "What we may call 'something there,' more deep and more general than any of the special and particular 'senses.'" Scripture offers less-than-perfectly-captured answers to questions that have no terminal answers, to which we can forever continue to find more and more without ever achieving "closure." They're mysteries.

Today we're more laudably humble before the mysterious real in scripture, at peace with the limitations of human perceptions, categories, and formulations.

Tradition

In contrast, for many Catholics, especially many in authority, tradition is rooted in stone. *Roma locuta, causa finita* (Rome has spoken, the case is closed) argues that once the Vatican has given an answer to a question—whether from the pope *ex cathedra,* in an encyclical, or through any office of his curia—loyal Catholics must yield will and judgment, even if the dictum contradicts everything they know from psychology, biology, physics, whatever. Denial—even expressing difficulty understanding—is tantamount to heterodoxy, if not heresy.

As Bishop Kenneth Untener wrote, "In the eyes of many people, the teaching church has committed a teacher's cardinal sin: it has become more concerned about itself than about the truth." He expands that insight into an apt analogy to maps drawn by early explorers which, over time, were changed and improved by later investigation. The terrain didn't change, but the maps did. But he continues, "The terrain no longer appears to be our issue. Our map is the issue."

Some church pronouncements have been not only out of focus but wrong—demonstrably, frequently, from the start. Most often (though it may take a century or two, and rarely as frank admission of error), the Spirit brings the church to her senses and she corrects the error.

Peter, the first pope, changed his mind radically on two questions he thought were essentials of the faith: circumcision and the dietary laws. Facing arguments of Paul—not a church "official"—

Peter admitted no one had to become a Jew before becoming an authentic Christian.

Paul also realized he'd been wrong taking Jesus literally about an imminent end. He told slaves to serve in fear and trembling and sent the slave Onesimus back to Philemon, but he was wrong—as Augustine was wrong believing slavery was part of the divine order. What gives me the right to challenge an apostle and a father of the church? The objective facts. The humanity of a slave is no more arguable than the toxicity of cyanide or the spherical shape of the earth.

For centuries church laws made Jews subhumans (however learned, generous, or pious). Not till Vatican II did Catholics stop referring to non-Catholic theists as "heretic, schismatic, infidel, and perfidious." Even Good Friday liturgy had "prayed" for them as *"animas diabolica fraude deceptas, haeretica pravitate deposita"* (souls deceived by hellish fraud, engendered by heretical depravity). The Second Vatican Council offered at least a tacit apology for centuries of inhumane error.

The church was not only wrong but criminally so in instituting and supporting the sale of indulgences, the Inquisition, and the crusades. Pius IX's *Syllabus of Errors* was an antihuman document that condemned civil education; freedom of speech, press, and religion; even moderate rationalism, Bible societies, liberal clerical groups—in short: challenge and growth. It imprisoned the church in a dungeon of anti-intellectualism, retrogression and suspicion for a hundred years till the gates were clanged open by the humane Pope John XXIII, who himself had been suspected of modernism when teaching at Bergamo. Now Francis lets the sunshine in.

Every child knows the earth goes around the sun, yet a papal commission met recently for twelve *years* to decide whether to exonerate Galileo. (Pope John Paul II gave in.) Such hesitance to admit mistakes not only doesn't shore up the church's authority but actually undermines it, when it also claims confession and resolution to amend are good for the souls of its members.

The only point worth making is, "We're still here! It's our family."

The Yen for Certitude

When I was studying what I then believed was philosophy (in Latin), I was mystified by what seemed celestial calculus. One thorny thesis in particular had twenty-three subdistinctions, and prying them apart left me feeling like Psyche sorting seeds. For a final term paper, I wrote about a *Summa* article in which Aquinas argued that all philosophy must ultimately be grounded back in concrete reality. I used a great deal from Cardinal Newman. When I got a C, I asked the prof why. His reply was terse: "Cardinal Newman was neither a philosopher *nor* a theologian." My numb reply was, "Then what am I doing here?" What the professor had meant, of course, was that Newman was neither a *scholastic* philosopher nor theologian.

Need for brain-surgeon precision in attempting to comprehend the incomprehensible has been with us since the first. Adam and Eve wanted to outsmart God. Can't be done. Such a desire for certitude and control is blasphemy. Oedipus, Faust, Hitler suffered few doubts. Nor has the church been free of that need to dominate the truth rather than submit to the truth—especially to the truth of our own limited minds. Take only two cases typical of many.

On Saturday, July 16, 1054, just before the afternoon liturgy, the delegate of the Roman pope strode into the Church of Santa Sophia in Constantinople and laid on the altar a bull excommunicating the Patriarch, the Eastern Emperor, and all their followers, then departed. Ostensibly, the major issue was the East's refusal to accept the word *filioque* ("and from the Son") into the Creed. The West believed the Holy Spirit did not proceed directly from the Father—as the Son did—but from the Father *and* the Son. The East accepted *"through"* the Son, but refused to "denigrate" the all-powerful Spirit to an inferior position. Thus, *half* the Christian church split from the other; each held the other in schism from itself. Over a single word, which the majority of believers—then and now—knew nothing about, could not explain, and couldn't care less about.

Think of how the certitudes in Islam have devastated our world today.

A second example: Charles V (whose main motive was the re-unification of Germany, not Christian doctrine) assembled representatives of Rome, Luther, Melanchthon, Calvin, and Zwingli and begged them to agree Jesus was at least *"somehow"* present more really in the Eucharist than in any other place. Luther believed in the real presence; Zwingli held a mere symbol; Calvin was somewhere between. The motives for recalcitrance were not doctrine but dominance.

For by far the majority of Christians the points at issue were mere theological lint picking. Aquinas himself confessed all our best efforts to put mysteries into formulas and all his insights into God were "straw" compared to the Reality.

At the beginning, the Christian way was never dialectic but always persuasion, not an attempt to out-argue the opposition—much less to silence or excommunicate them from dialogue. Jesus' own parable of the wheat and the weeds declared unequivocally that if evil can't be uprooted without harm to the good, we must tolerate the "evil." We don't throw out the bent reed or quench the smoldering flax.

Could anyone be converted—or sustained in it—by a *Summa*? I by no means belittle intellectual investigation of truths of the faith. Rather I question what can become a tyranny of the intellect over the heart. Theologizing Christianity always must be checked back to Christ himself. Conversion of goals and values was the heart of Jesus' message, not comprehension.

What we call the Apostles' Creed wasn't written by the apostles, and they would probably have been mystified if asked to explain its various parts. Yet somehow they managed to begin a crusade that has lasted two millennia.

Beyond that, what the honest, intelligent Catholic wants is a study of theological and moral doctrine that focuses somewhere between patriarchal (or fundamentalist) certitude, on the one hand, and existential *angoisse*, on the other.

Tradition and Evolution

Like oak roots under pavement, so many natural forces

work inexorably—however slowly—against inflexible traditions. Their promise of security can't resist the needs of the human spirit.

The objective configuration of the cosmos forced the church, after centuries, to realize we had to go back and revise our scriptural certitudes, from Eden to the Ascension, to the nature of heaven and hell. The objective nature of human beings must force us to accept that no one, not even the church, can legitimately treat humans like cattle or adults like children. What Father would want his children to remain infants—much less sheep? The will of God manifest in nature and scripture is for growth, change, renewal: creation moved from inanimate to vegetative to animal to human; the two Testaments show God coming back again and again, saying, "All right, now let's start over, better this time"; the whole gospel message—culminating on Easter Sunday—is rebirth. Not merely change but *metanoia*: total reversal of our certitudes and expectations.

In his inaugural speech in the Nazareth synagogue after the desert temptations, Jesus announced his platform, not only for his own public ministry but for the church: "The Spirit of the Lord is upon me, because he has chosen me to bring good news to the poor. He has sent me to proclaim *liberty* to captives and *recovery of sight* to the blind, to set *free* the oppressed and announce the *amnesty* of God" (Luke 4:18–19). And in John's gospel, Jesus says, "If you obey my teaching, you are really my disciples; you will know the truth, and the truth will set you *free*" (8:31). The objective truth—however unnerving and challenging to our former certitudes—can never harm genuine Christianity. Truth can't contradict truth.

Throughout her history, the teaching church learned from non-Catholic sources initially held suspect: Plato, Aristotle, and their Muslim commentators. She learned slowly to rethink and understand herself better from those who challenged her: Galileo, Luther, Freud, Darwin, Protestant biblical critics. In contrast, documents like the new *Catechism* disdain enrichment from psychology, biology, sociology, feminism, and surely not socialism or Marxism. To some critics, the church seems secure, proving herself *by* herself. There's so much more she could rely on!

Although Jesus was (in our terms) a "layman" in his religion, he didn't hesitate to make a quite dramatic statement in clearing out the Temple. He didn't hesitate to "correct" Moses himself. Jesus never strongly rebuked a sexual sinner; in fact, the only sinners he did rail at—fiercely—were the clergy, the hypocrisy of the priests of his own religion and the materialist ambitions of his own future priests.

Disputed Questions

I am not empowered to give secure answers to the questions I raise here, not being a professional theologian or a Vatican official. But I am empowered to raise the questions, even ill-advised ones, as Peter, James, and John (and their mother!), and Thomas did to Jesus.

Since Jesus, when asked who is the first in the Kingdom, raised up a child, I wonder what Jesus would say about the need for infant baptism—at least to relieve the burden of sin from a person not yet capable of responsibility even for his or her own toilet habits. Since he worked in a culture where it was unthinkable for a woman to be even an expert in the law, not to mention a priest, I wonder if the Jesus who chose women as the privileged first witnesses of his resurrection would have chosen the twelve differently today. Aquinas and Augustine agree Jesus shared Eucharist with Judas, which makes me wonder how Jesus would react to someone who sought Communion but was divorced and remarried. I wonder what the Jesus who dealt so blithely with the much-wed Samaritan woman would say about the relative claims of ova and sperm against those of two loving, good-souled, and committed parents. I am even tempted to wonder what Jesus would say to two lifelong companions of the same sex who must live a life they surely would not have chosen for themselves. It's a wonder-full life.

A canon law prof asked a seminarian what he'd tell a divorced couple asking Communion; the younger man said, "Well, I'd try to handle it as Jesus would." The canon lawyer exploded!

"Come One, Come All!"

The word "catholic" means at its roots "universal, broad-based, eclectic, liberal, latitudinarian." That was drummed into us as kids—*even though*, equally loud and much clearer, we heard warnings about how quickly and *completely* we would be cut off from God by one single mortal sin. It's unfair, but in my seminary moral and canon law classes, we seemed to spend an inordinate amount of time studying grounds for excommunication and for withholding absolution. When Jesus was so profligate with forgiveness.

Many who can't tolerate ambiguity and gray areas, suggest that if your grown kids stop attending Mass, they won't make it into heaven. They seem to overlook the testimony from Jesus himself that Abraham, Isaac, and Jacob are at the heavenly banquet but were never even baptized. Gandhi missed Mass his whole life, but I can't imagine God blackballing him. Nor could I worship a God less tolerant than I am. Those who predict God's moves about the afterlife say those folks will be admitted only because they never knew any better—which scuttles all chances for those who *had* Catholic tutelage. And yet the first pope denied Christ vehemently, with oaths, and still was accepted back. "Oh, yes," they'll say. "But they repented *before* their deaths!" Yet, at least to my mind, the resurrection of Jesus proves pretty clearly death is no restraint on what God can do. As Mrs. Patty Crowley on the pope's birth control commission asked, "Father, do you believe God follows all your orders?"

In his lifetime, with scandalous tolerance, Jesus insisted on consorting with whores, tax collectors, lepers, and various others whose company we ourselves would prefer to avoid. I'm left with the suspicion Jesus wasn't as fastidious as most of *us* might be. Then there's The Twelve he personally chose—ham-fisted and often ham-headed, including a collaborationist tax collector, an embezzler who sold him, and a fair-weather boaster. All of them missing Jesus at every turn! I'm left with the conclusion Jesus as "The Gate" to eternal life is much broader, less nit picking than the hawk-eyed border guards whom well-meaning folks taught me to envision.

The constriction of the so-called narrow gate seems redesigned from the original come-one, come-all notion suggested by the promiscuity of the original Formulator. The thief crucified next to Jesus merely took pity on what he probably saw as a deluded fellow sufferer, and he got a free pass. In Matthew's description of the last judgment, our scarlet sins don't even seem to enter into the proceedings. "I was hungry. I was thirsty. What did you do for me?" It seems the only passport you need at "The Gate" is a habit of being kind to the unlovely. And yet I was told for so long getting into heaven was like scoring a goal: having one foot or another body part and the slightest part of the ball over the line. *Before* the final whistle!

It was left to the nitpickers and distinction makers and quality experts and time-study men and Pharisees and witch hunters to turn the good news of life and freedom into a prison of rules. *All* the laws, without exception, are bound up in *loving*—which seals up all loopholes and evasions and pharisaic distinctions embedded in every negative "Thou shalt not." Love—truly, selflessly *love*—and you'll be grateful to serve the God who's our source of existence. You'll honor your parents, others' property and bodies, others' right to your truthfulness. If you can be "convicted" of truly, selflessly loving, you *can't* be convicted of *anything* else.

Each us squeezed into existence through an orifice any mother will testify was far too constricted for the task. Yet we all did make it. If the scriptures—and also the millennial history of God's evolution—testify anything about God, it's God's unquenchable softheartedness for the unlikely, the ones who hang on despite the odds.

If you're openhearted, compassionate, forgiving, you've *nothing* to fear. Nothing. Ever.

Were Jesus to come back today, he would not expect the bush to look even remotely like the mustard seed he planted. But one can pray he would say, "Yes. I guess that's, more or less, pretty much, what I had in mind. All right, now let's. . . ."

21.
Beyond Authorities

When I was a child, I spoke like a child,
I thought like a child, I reasoned like a child.
When I became an adult, I put an end to
childish ways.

—1 Corinthians 13:11

In a few confessions, penitents (sounding, at a guess, over sixty) claimed "disobeying my parents." They were sincere, though their parents long ago departed to the bosom of Abraham. They weren't regretting selling short their own sacredness or their friendship with God but disobeying a *rule*, betraying their superego parent, enthroned somewhere in their souls like a jowly Dickensian judge. Similar confessions convince me others still hold the organized church in the same unquestionable eminence—even when its decrees stand in direct conflict with just about everything else an adult Catholic knows to be true. As the Clarence Darrow character says in *Inherit the Wind*, "The Bible's a book. It's a good book. But it's not the *only* book." No genuine Catholic can ignore the authoritative voice of the church. But as St. John Paul II wrote, "Truth cannot contradict truth."

Most churchgoing Catholics have faced that conflict regarding artificial birth control and finally felt the freedom to differ—as honest, well-informed adults. But last year after Mass, a man taxed me—roundly—when I said at the consecration, "This is a cup of my blood . . . which will be shed for you and for *all*." He was going to write to the archbishop—and the pope—about what he called my "disobedience." When he said "pope," I knew he was bluffing. But his riled righteousness was fierce. Even though he was acting childish: "*I'm* gonna tell *Dad* on you!"

Being an independent-thinking adult Catholic is far—far—more complex and difficult than lockstep obedience. Simpler to remain a child. Or a sheep. Back then, The Church Taught were illiterate peasants with nothing to teach, and The Church Teaching believed they had nothing left to learn. That's changed since the rise of the middle class when learning leaked out of the monasteries. The American church connived in that egalitarianism by heroic sacrifice to bring immigrant kids beyond literacy. Now, people in the pews often have more potent educations than their pastor. Or even their bishop. An insult to deny their evident *expertise.*

Everything we discern about the natural process of human maturation is a progress from dependency to autonomy, losing the training wheels, using our minds to assume control of our souls into our own better-informed, experienced hands. We're missioned by our designer to assume the throne of self-governance.

"Know Thyself"

> *Know and obey the rules well, so you will know how*
> *to break them properly.*
> —Fourteenth Dalai Lama

Developmental psychologists like Piaget, Kohlberg, and Gilligan have mapped out a reliable scheme of moral (human) growth in three levels of increasing awareness of the realities and challenges of life—level one: the fractious child; level two: the level-headed adolescent; level three: the autonomous soul. Consequently, each surge in awareness opens a broader inner sense of responsibility and competence as one matures. Or it ought to. Although it might be a tad too instructional, this chapter makes that inbred invitation explicit.

First, the healthy young animal stage of childhood (the Freudian id, preconventional, self-centered motives). Second, into the middle level: adolescence (inner parent, conventional limits on behavior, a Freudian superego of dos and don'ts). From that level a person *can* evolve into a third level of autonomous adulthood, a personally validated, genuine self. The individual who does achieve that adult level has rational powers and the perspective of experience to critique both the demands of the first-level animal in us (id) and the second-level restraints imposed by adapting to the rights of others (superego). Then a natural *invitation* (not automatic) is to rise *beyond* conformity to others' rules, others' scriptural experiences, others' dogmas into what Richard Rohr, OFM, calls "The True Self." Or not.

Anyone interested in this particular book quite likely ought to have already left behind (mostly) both the self-centered demands of the bottom level, as well as the dictated governance of the middle level, and become engaged in the challenges of that third level: adult self-possession.

Those psychologists further differentiate within each of those three major levels two separate progressive *stages* in each, and most adults can look back at them like a family photo album and say, "Yeah. I was there." Remembering the lessons to this point will not only help to understand who we've become but will also give us insights into our own grandchildren.

The scheme is also helpful in understanding "grown-ups" who seem stranded still in early stages, as yet to lay claim to honest adulthood. They never had the time, inclination, or impetus from outside to discover and own a soul, a self. They whine like caged animals ("Managers always hate me!"), use cunning to slither through loopholes ("I did *not* have sex with that woman!"), cling to bumper-sticker ideas ("Stop them taking our jobs!"), refuse to drop barriers between "us" and "them" ("We must retaliate against *some* Arabs!"). Their schooling failed to teach them how to think honestly for themselves.

Each of the three levels (child, parent, adult) splits into two upwardly moving stages.

The bottom first stage of the preconventional-id-child level (even in physical adults) is motivated almost exclusively by animal *fear*; what will this cost me—or hurt me least? For such immature people—no matter their age—the equality of human beings is as far from their minds as spherical geometry. The "ordinary folks" who managed Nazi extermination camps chose to inhumanly abuse human beings every day rather than possible death on the Russian front. They choose "accepted" options because if they don't, Mom'll get mad, they'll fail the course, go to jail, be excommunicated, end up in hell. Even at age seventy!

The second stage of that bottom preconventional level has a mildly improved motive: hope of *reward*. It is, indeed, one step up the evolutionary scale, not just to escape pain but some shrewd hope of recompense for doing "the right thing." Enlightened self-interest. When Nixon said on the tapes, "That would be wrong," often he meant, "We couldn't get away with that." They choose "right" options just to get a cookie, pass, merit a raise, be elected, sing in heaven.

Both of these stages could apply as well to beasts in the circus (the whip and the treat) as well as to people who had human parents but have yet to comprehend how humans differ from other animals. At least from the 1930s through the 1950s, that's about as far as religious education went. Hell and heaven. Nothing about personal integrity, and pride was the root of *all* sins. Any further religious maturity was left to the individual and to by guess and by golly.

Maturing onto the next major level, the conventional, is in fact a quantum leap upward and outward, beyond the cramped limits of one's own selfishness into loyalty—on stage three, to the small group (family, school, team, gang, platoon), and then on stage four, loyalty to the laws that control and protect "society" (neighborhood, city, country, church).

Level two moves beyond *self*-centeredness. The radius of human awareness, concern, and sacrifice broadens out so that I'll offer the same intensity of commitment I have for myself to these others whom I've willingly grappled to myself in my support group. A huge development from personal protectiveness and acquisitiveness. At stage three the scope of awareness and care extends beyond the self to an approved circle. Stage four reaches far broader groups, even people one will never meet: law and order. It's the Golden Rule (which appears almost verbatim in every philosophy since the caves) to do unto others—beyond those chosen few at stage three—as I would do unto myself (level one). This wider viewpoint asks, "What would happen if everybody . . . ?" However, it's not totally unbiased. If my brother were dealing drugs—even to grade-school children—I might be more likely to lie to the police for him. They will worship because it's "good for the family" and bail out the ne'er-do-well brother-in-law for my sister's sake. But don't expect me to do the same for Mexicans who paddled the Rio Grande.

This fourth live-and-let-live stage "fits" the profile evolved in *Soul Searching*, a national study of American young people's grasp of religious realities: "moralistic therapeutic deism." There has to be a God to explain "a lotta stuff" but as irrelevant to daily life as other UFOs. That is, religion fosters subjective well-being and lubricates relationships. God loves us, but doesn't expect too much beyond not hurting people. God is to help people succeed in life, make them feel good, and help them get along with others. Sort of the fairy godmother at the other end of a 911 number. The study claims the least religiously involved young people are Catholics and the greatest influence shaping their "beliefs" is their parents.

Level three, the highest, is postconventional. Christianity is at its very core postconventional. It goes *beyond* not only self-interest but beyond the laws and customs of family-community-nation-church. If all the rent-a-cops went on strike, they would *not* park in the handicapped slots or spit gum in a drinking fountain or leave the toilet roll empty. This is beyond the simplicity that officials depend on: "My country (family-ethnic community-church) right or wrong." On the contrary, if any object of my allegiance is wrong, I feel impelled to stand up and challenge it.

It's difficult to differentiate the two stages here on level three, but one norm might be the *abrasiveness* of the person who's achieved it. Young Jane Fonda was completely sincere in opposing the inhumanity of the Vietnam War. She—quite selflessly—risked a lucrative career that depended on public approval. She had a wider, more sensitive appreciation of what "humanity" means than those who called Vietnamese "gooks" or used "pacification" to refer to wiping a village off the face of the earth. *But* she did pull off pretty dumb things, which soured her own appeal. Not a few staunch Catholics still have no recollection of her humanity, only her "disloyalty" during a shameful war. Now she's matured, she herself seems to admit that.

This stage could be misread as anarchy, but nothing could be less true. On one hand, it admits some laws are immoral, groundless, like justifying slavery. But the larger difference is the motive for choice. Not that an act is "illegal," but it's out-and-out *wrong*, like Nazi racial laws. There is an objective human norm higher than codified civil or religious law. Jesus was a perfect example of that.

Nor is there disdain for the previous stages—without which this level of moral integrity would be inaccessible. Those were like the first stage of a rocket to be jettisoned, not because it has no value but that there's no longer need for it. One's motivation has *nothing* to do *anymore* with parents or "socialization" or superego or "society" or police. In a riot, such self-possessed people wouldn't merely disdain heisting a TV from a broken store window but would likely stand in the street begging people to come to their senses and go home.

The psychologists all admit few reach the sixth stage—the serene soul. Francis of Assisi, Catherine of Siena, Thomas More, Abraham Lincoln, Gandhi, Jackie Robinson, Mother Teresa, Mandela—none faultless, but each exponents of a humanity few of us can aspire to. Their root motivation seems to be, "I will do the right thing and refuse the wrong thing, even if you kill me."

None of the stages or levels depends on IQ or formal education. The key is *perspective*, breadth of awareness, and depth of concern. It took a certain "genius" to eliminate fifteen million *Untermenchen* under the Nazi regime, while many illiterates on their walk to the gas chambers showed more profound nobility of spirit than the clever ones who orchestrated their annihilation.

This schema is "handy," no more. Laudably humanistic, but even stage six isn't *quite* Christian. Devotees of Jesus Christ go light years beyond justice and debts. They *love* people they "ought" to hate. Jesus' admonition is a given: "Love your enemies . . . lend, expecting nothing in return . . . for [our Father] is kind to the ungrateful and the selfish" (Luke 6:25). In *Les Miz*, Bishop Bienvenu gives Jean Valjean not only the silverware he's stolen but two silver candlesticks he's overlooked. That's way beyond justice. That's Jesus. That's us.

The only reason I've burdened the reader with this overly

"academic" intrusion is the hope that it will remove any shame or guilt (or fear of hell) that might arise in middle-aged Catholics for daring to trust their own honest judgment even when it conflicts with the "official church." We have to remember God gave us intelligence long (long) before he saw need to give us the Magisterium. Job and Jeremiah show God has no objection—much less any sanction—when humans rise up and rail even against *him*, much less his employees! Jacob got the name "Israel" because it means "*wrestler* with God." If we cling to "My church, right or wrong," we betray our founder who laid about his own Temple in a rage and called its hierarchy such uncomplimentary (not to say "heretical" or even "suicidal") names as "hypocrites, blind guides, fools, tombs filled with rot, tangle of snakes, fit for hell." The entire history of Judaism and Christianity calls on us to continue to evolve. So does the will of God evident in cosmology and evolution. The divine impulse is deniable but inescapable. Evolve or die. (Often before need of burial.)

Jesus admired the pagan woman (Matthew 15:37) who sparred with him about her daughter being worth the scraps from privileged children's tables. She reminds me (perhaps Jesus, too) of Abraham when Yahweh was about to blast Sodom and Gomorrah. "But if we can find even a hundred just people?" And he keeps going till he's down to ten, then even just one. But neither Yahweh nor Jesus seemed to mind. It impels me to urge adult Catholics to outgrow childish ways.

Vatican II was one more quantum leap for the Catholic Church in understanding individual freedom. In the wake of the freedom and literacy unleashed by the Renaissance, the Reformation, the Enlightenment, and national revolutions from monarchical domination, the official church still clung like a shipwreck victim to its sovereignty over the individual conscience. Pius IX (1846–78) condemned abstract religious liberty as moral relativism, and he held that error has no rights. His *Syllabus of Errors* forbade independence of Roman approval. Catholicism should be the religion of the state; no one should be free to choose a religion. Asserting such rights deserves excommunication. That was the Catholic Church I was born and raised in. As a condition of ordination, every priest candidate had to swear an oath against such modernist heresies. I did myself in 1963 (with my fingers crossed. Truly!).

But Vatican II (1962–65), not without infighting, adopted a new stance on religious freedom, more realistic in the face of pervasive pluralism. Pope Paul personally insisted the declaration on religious freedom be brought to a preliminary vote, where it was overwhelmingly approved, 1,997 to 224. "The right to the exercise of freedom, especially in religious and moral matters, is an inalienable requirement of the dignity of man."

Thomas Aquinas had insisted that a person must follow his or her reasoned conscience, even if it turns out to be objectively erroneous. And Cardinal Newman put it pithily: "I shall drink to the Pope, if you please. Still, to conscience first, and to the Pope afterwards."

Far be it from me to raise mutinous thoughts among the faithful. On the contrary, I'd just like to becalm any discomfort at the other end of the spectrum when, almost unbidden, resentment surges up in them about official church inflexibility. That uneasiness is in no way schismatic or secessionist. Uncountable saints have resorted to it. Not only understandable and acceptable, but all these scriptural facts indicate that standing up—even to God—is pretty clearly admirable. In fact, expected of us by our God-designed intelligent human nature.

What at least seems undeniable from this mountain of evidence is that the restless God—who pestered the reluctant Abraham and Sarah, Moses, Isaiah, Jeremiah, Simon Peter—is calling anyone over fifty to shift our attitudes beyond fear, beyond mere hope of reward, beyond even our amply proven love of family, beyond law and order to a new mode of connection between God and our world. He asks us to grasp a coherent overall posture, which the ages have always called "wisdom," and to lay hold of an unswerving sense of an integral soul prepared to face eternity.

That gives me a certain, well, let's call it "lessening of apprehension," when I'm trying to decide what to do at Communion during a marriage between a Catholic and an Anglican, or just two gays living together, or a loving couple once married to two other still-living people.

Serpents and Doves

"Take up your bed and walk as an adult" accepts the fact (obvious from *every* other source) that one is no longer a child. And never was a sheep. We must accept its legitimacy: We're grown-ups. And seasoned. And reliable. Then—among other things—finding something worth standing up for rather than just against.

Astuteness and sophistication and personally owned responsibility are templates of genuine adulthood. However, adulthood is not automatic the way puberty was. It takes effort. Nor is experience the best teacher—automatically. Only experience reflected on: taken apart, evaluated, reassembled into a personally forged worldview/conscience/philosophy/theology. That requires the skills of *critical thinking*—which are hardly the accepted task of formal education, but which most of us have learned, despite that lack, by the seat of our pants.

That call for astute perception and evaluation seems to belie Jesus' demand we become children to find the gate to the Kingdom. Not so. He invites us to use the finer-honed powers of the experienced, learned adult in *service* of the childlike impulse to run into the arms of strangers. All our lives we've been pummeled with "the dove" motives—just as we've been conditioned to the Holy Spirit fluttering rather than sternly commanding the chaos of the creation to line up with the laws of gravity, electromagnetism, and relativity, and even more often by restricting Jesus to the shepherd rather than the storm silencer and hound of the hypocrites.

The task of the grown-up has always been not to forge an uneasy *detente* between exuberance and control, but to bring about a *marriage* of the two, a comfortable fusion in which, like the two contrary prongs of a fused magnet, they create a third power that neither has alone: the soul. (There's an insight there, too, into the Trinity in whose image we are made.)

In too simplistic pictures of the lion lying down with the lamb, the lion has always become a cute pussycat, contentedly licking the sweet lamb. As Chesterton said, such pictures show a rank imperialism on the part of the lamb—devouring the lion rather than vice versa. The lion has to lie down with the lamb without losing his leonine ferocity. (Witness Jesus with the Pharisees, the money changers, his self-possession with Pilate, the scourgers, the Calvary crowd.)

Unless our Catholicism is still like the knickers and pinafores that used to be suitable, we ought not only to have an inner freedom, decisiveness, authority, and integrity no young person has had wherewithal to achieve, but we ought to have those qualities in a way others can *see*.

In our present lives, there are places where a priest in a collar would be as welcome and comfortable as a skunk at a garden party. The watercooler, lunchroom, bowling alley, cocktail party, airplane ride. There are times no priest is even present to challenge a racial slur, a sexual insensitivity. That's what baptism ordained you for: to listen, to heal, to invite, to offer understanding and forgiveness.

Hell and purgatory are (thank God) getting less play as motives. They were lowest-level incentives anyway. Now we have to show we've evolved *beyond* the motives of heaven and hell, and we're trying to lure others along that same spectrum of motives—ultimately to "I couldn't live with myself if I did that." That will take more creativity—more sensitivity—than the church or many other societies have shown in the past.

Just as doctors and lawyers have to consistently keep up on new rulings and new pharmaceuticals, or else become ineffective, so, too, the genuine Catholic. A lot of meaningful, challenging new insights have been busting out all over since we were in college. Try *The Tablet, America, Commonweal,* and for the venturesome, *The National Catholic Reporter.* It's a sure bet at least a dozen couples in a parish would welcome an invitation to a book club.

If one exists, the devil trembles in terror at people who laugh, especially from down in the belly. If you feel bedeviled, you have no need of a priest in a surplice with holy water and a Roman ritual. The most effective exorcism is an unflagging smile. Prove me wrong! I dare you!

We are not going to change the whole world, but we can change ourselves and feel free as birds. We can be se-

rene even in the midst of calamities and, by our serenity, make others more tranquil. Serenity is contagious. If we smile at someone, he or she will smile back. And a smile costs nothing. We should   plague everyone with joy. If we are to die in a minute, why not die happily, laughing?
—Swami Satchidananda

22.
Spendthrift Forgiveness

Who am I to judge?

—Pope Francis I

On the evening of November 14, 1940, 515 German bombers flew over Coventry, a city in the British midlands, obliterating a third of the factories, and most of what was left of city buildings and homes. Coventry Cathedral was hit by incendiaries and devoured in a firestorm.

After the war, when the cathedral was rebuilt, a gutted side chapel was kept—empty steel frames from stained-glass windows, an altar made from rubble, a rude cross made from two rough blackened timbers, and across the window wall only two shocking words: "Father forgive."

There you have a great deal of what Christianity means in just two words.

My college roommate's sister had five children, and one Saturday evening one of her girls came from a parish dance with a pack of kids. One boy invited them in to see his father's guns. One went off and shattered my friend's daughter's head. Beyond all reason, her parents asked the boy to be one of their daughter's pallbearers. Does that make any sense to you at all?

One Sunday morning my dad's partner fled town with his wife and daughters—and the entire business bank account. And Dad refused to prosecute. Why? "I don't want those two girls growing up knowing their father's a convict." Can you make any sense at all of that?

When I use Dad's story in class to show the abyss between justice and Christianity, kids who've had what they call ten to fifteen *years* of Christian brainwashing snort in *disbelief*. "That guy's gonna go out and do it again and again! . . . Shoulda thought of his own daughters. . . . Your dad was no businessman." That's undeniable. Some values were more precious to Dad than business. More important than *justice*. Not educated, but I think he was a saint. (If that means anything.)

When I was their age, when it happened, I didn't understand either. I thought Dad was a sucker. Which, of course, he was. At the time, I was too dumb to know real courage. I'd been baptized—and fully brainwashed to Catholicism. But I'd never really been *converted*.

Despite catechisms, Masses, novenas, I was as pagan as the next kid. No more truly Christian than some fifth-century Saxon brute booted to the baptism line by his chief: part of the surrender. No more than anyone who writes "Catholic" next to "religion" when he's no more still a Catholic than he's still a Boy Scout.

This book is a chance to ask—only yourself—whether after all these years of faithful Catholic practice you're genuinely Christian yet, whether you've ever been *converted*. If you've been personally staggered to realize the absolute *only* question about your Christian life has nothing—*nothing*—to do with sin. Only *kindness*: empathy, healing, forgiveness. "I was hungry . . . thirsty . . . naked . . . sick . . . in prison" (Matthew 25). Kindness given only because of the victim's need.

I don't think my Catholic training had much to do with kindness: just guilt and atonement.

The gospel core is surrender—a repugnant notion now in marketplace, academe, athletics, entertainment, journalism. A culture of narcissism. Few lifelong Catholics are stunned by the contrast between what they accept uncritically all week as determinant values and what they claim to profess for one hour a week at Mass.

The innermost Christian doctrine is that the son of God "*emptied* himself"—gave up all privileges to become helpless as we are. He was stripped, scourged to the bone, spiked to a cross, and hung there three hours while soldiers and priests and ordinary passersby mocked him for the loser he surely was. First thing he said when they got him up there was, "Father, forgive them. They don't know what they're doing." Can you *believe* that? If not, your Christian label may be only slapped onto the surface, like the black smudge on Ash Wednesday.

That haunted me when I was fired a few years ago—the assumption that a real Christian holds no grudges. I couldn't say the "Our Father" anymore because I literally choked when I said, "as we forgive those who trespass against us." It was rank hypocrisy. Because I was seething with resentment—in the very act of praying. So I had to write and forgive the men who did it or else stop attending Mass. I still despise them, but I forgave them. That's at least a start. Loving is quite separate from liking. If you're human, I suspect there's someone about whom you still say in the depths of your soul, "I could never forgive them. *Never!*"

You'll never find peace with a fist full of a grudge. Imagine you were to be crucified tomorrow and had a chance to wash their feet. Jesus did that to Judas, and—according to Augustine and Aquinas—Jesus shared Eucharist with him, too.

Before you say, "I'm Christian," again, prudent to ask if you really mean *that*.

The Longtime Christian Motive, Attitude, Goal

> For I am convinced that neither death, nor life, nor angels, nor rulers, nor things present, nor things to come, nor powers, nor height, nor depth, nor anything else in all creation, will be able to separate us from the love of God in Christ Jesus our Lord.
>
> —Romans 8:38–39

Anyone trained Catholic in the 1930s, 1940s, and 1950s rarely heard that declaration of God's helpless, unconditional love. We received a catechesis mediated through well-meaning Pharisees, bean counters, budget balancers. They were fine, kind human beings, unwittingly enslaved to an economic metaphor of our relationship to God. It had nothing to do with fatherhood (even if most of them were called "Father"). Instead, we bowed to an overwhelming debt incurred by the first rebellious humans. (Even though it was God who gave them freedom to do it and foresaw they would.) Few dared ask how an alleged "all-loving" God could hold a grudge 30,000 years when his Son told us we shabby humans must forgive 490 times. Each. I can't recall questioning an indelible stain bequeathed to every baby because of eating just one piece of fruit. We also uncritically accepted that God withheld forgiveness until his Son crept down and endured an utterly ghastly passion and death to pay the debt and convince his loving Father to relent.

Even then—even when we heard and accepted the total defeat of evil on the cross and the instant availability of forgiveness if we honestly asked our prodigal Father for it—we were instructed to be ever vigilant, fleeing the virulent contagion of sin. We were to be especially wary of "pride," since God would rather we be mediocre than vain. Then—even if we managed to dance through that minefield for a lifetime, and even if we had insurance of the last rites, the accountants dreamed up a satanically clever further threat: "the temporal punishment due to sin." Confession and a firm purpose of amendment got rid only of the *reatus culpae* (state of *guilt*), but not the *reatus poenae* (state of *liability*). Even after one had confessed with total sincerity, even after a purportedly all-loving God had forgiven, there was still the punishment to be "paid." In a quid pro quo, strict-justice worldview, you might be—technically—"forgiven," but you still had to "pay up" with suffering in purgatory until your friends and relatives bailed you out of debtors' prison.

That was one costly piece of fruit! Jesus interpreted by Ebenezer Scrooge.

The new *Catechism* (1997) insists that Vatican II did nothing official to shift that understanding of the escalating cost of forgiveness for personal sin.

> Grave sin deprives us of communion with God and therefore makes us incapable of eternal life, the privation of which is called the "eternal punishment" of sin. On the other hand every sin, even venial, entails an unhealthy attachment to creatures, which must be purified either here on earth, or after death in the state called Purgatory. This purification frees one from what is called the "temporal punishment" of sin. . . . The for-

giveness of sin and restoration of communion with God entail remission of eternal punishment sin; temporal punishment remains.

At least in my own personal grasp of that doctrine as a child and young man, it wasn't I who closed the door of "communion with God" but God—who found me so detestable he wanted nothing to do with me till I'd cleaned up my act. And even then, my "welcome" back was sheerly *conditional*. Ready to be whipped away at the slightest deviation from righteousness. For bean counters, unconditional love simply would not compute. It was irrational. Which is unarguably true. An unredeemed cynic in me wonders if those who formed those doctrines had ever truly experienced what any kind of love means.

One could conclude that the deepest *motive* for being Christian is fear of punishment, that the Christian *attitude* was one of constant vigilance, that the Christian *goal* is eluding hell and, as my mother put it up to the time of her death, "just catching hold of heaven with my fingernails."

She was a steadfast, long-suffering, dutiful Catholic. But I think when she wanted love, assurance, companionship, understanding, she bypassed God and went to the Blessed Mother.

How many of us achieved a more civilized, adult, Christian understanding?

Except for vague notions of "easing up" of what "Catholic" means that we gathered from the secular press back around Vatican II, and maybe a rare homily suggesting more than mere dutifulness ("Pay, pray, obey"), what has amplified most middle-aged Catholics' souls? Their person-to-person connection with God? As I said, I can't remember a single theology professor—or even a homilist—ever saying, "When I pray." I at least can't recall anyone impressing on me that God loves me as helplessly as a mother loves her child on death row.

Did they forbear to tell us about unconditional love because they feared we'd run amok with our God-given freedom? If so, I have to admit that it really did work as efficiently and effectively and uncritically as modern commercials engender and feed infantile greed.

The Original Motive, Attitude, and Goal

The gospel evidence seems to establish the original *motive* of Christianity (starting from the summons of the first disciples) was being *called*, despite evident flaws. That the consistent *attitude* offered by Jesus was *trust* in him and in his Father. And that the *goal* was always "eternal life"—not restricted, as the common insight seems, just to squeeze into eternal bliss with the fires of hell licking at our heels—but understood as Jesus himself described his intention in coming here:

—"I came that they may have life, and have it more abundantly." (John 10:10)

—"Forgive, and you will be forgiven; give, and it will be given to you. A good measure, pressed down, shaken together, running over, will be put into your lap; for the measure you give will be the measure you get back." (Luke 6:37–38)

—"Those who eat my flesh and drink my blood have [present tense] eternal life." (John 6:54)

—"I am the way, and the truth, and the life." (John 14:6)

Lot of exuberance there. Maybe I slept through classes about that. Hard to imagine, though, I dozed selectively through just the exhilarating stuff for thirty years of Catholic theology.

Cosmology, evolution, human development, almost every story of Yahweh/Trinity in the Hebrew and Christian scriptures. Heal. Start over.

All those sources seem to challenge the *Catechism*'s assertion sin "deprives us of communion with God," since Yahweh is so often pictured as Israel's husband waiting patiently outside her whorehouse for her to come to her senses. It belies the patience of the prophets. It overlooks Jesus' almost embarrassing infatuation with sinners. Nor is there any attempt I could find that faces the conflict between the claim that we must take the means to purify *ourselves* in contrast to the doctrine that Jesus' death on the cross took care of that *for* us—provided we're humble enough to accept his kind forgiveness and *exoneration*.

Still more determinative of what "Christian" means for an adult is the invariant habits of Jesus dealing with individual sinners one on one. It is totally in the other direction from the too-easy-to-hand economic metaphor of the *Catechism,* and that underlies at least my recollection of my Catholic indoctrination. Never once does Jesus force a sinner to crawl, never once does he ask for a catalogue of sins by species and number, never once does he exact a retributive penance (in this world or in the next). Even "heretics" had gentler treatment from Jesus than they could expect from the later traditional church. According to the parable of the weeds (Matthew 13:24–30), they should be left as they are until the harvest.

Jesus' irritation at religious teachers is so frequent it's a wonder our instructors could have ignored it. What's common to these "clerical" offenders is their consistent refusal to see anything wrong with their suppositions, no sense of a need for repentance, since the rectitude of their convictions was unquestionable to them. The problem was never their sins but the narcissism that refused to admit them.

Something of the same has taken place—unwittingly, I suspect—in the catechesis that's replaced the vindictive economy we learned. In reaction to that un-Christian Christianity, the pendulum has rocketed in the opposite direction—where the whole concept of "sin" seems now to have been abandoned. In "softening up" the Lion of Judah, they've rendered him impotent. Most products of religious education now insist, "Guilt trips are bad for you." They've never been told that without guilt, we get extermination camps, drive-by shootings, date rape.

Jesus mentions sins aplenty: "fornication, theft, murder, adultery, greed, maliciousness, deceit, sensuality, envy, blasphemy, arrogance, an obtuse spirit" (Mark 8:21–22). He was not as blasé about sin as nominal Christians like to believe.

But Jesus also offered forgiveness aplenty. When Peter asked how many times, "seventy times seven times," and if God expects as much of us, we can expect at least as much of God. Though sinless himself, Jesus had a remarkable empathy for weakness. "The bruised reed he will not crush; the smoldering wick he will not quench" (Matthew 12:20). "I give you my word, every sin will be forgiven humankind and all the blasphemies they utter, but whoever blasphemes against the Holy Spirit will never be forgiven"

(Mark 3:28–29). Perhaps that enigmatic, sole unforgivable sin is despair, but a case could also be made for its being "an obtuse spirit," impregnable even to the Spirit's movement suggesting something is amiss and needs forgiving. Or even less understandable, that we are still loved even in sin.

The key—as so many gospel parables show—is opening the eyes, submitting to the cure of our blindness. Jesus did not come to hawk guilt but to offer freedom. As he said in his inauguration "platform" in the Nazareth synagogue, he was sent to declare the year of God (Luke 4:16–19): unconditional *amnesty* for those willing to *avail* themselves of it. The *only* requisite—in the moral practice of Jesus—was admitting one's need of it.

The Woman Known as a Sinner (Luke 7:36–50). As they dined, a woman "known in town as a sinner" entered, stood at Jesus' couch, weeping. She wiped the tears from his feet with her hair, kissing them. His host fumed; if Jesus was a prophet, he'd know what kind of woman this was. *His* rectitude was at stake, not her shame. But Jesus said, "I tell you why her sins are forgiven—because of her great love. Little is forgiven those whose love is small." The woman said *nothing*. She merely came to Jesus, humbled herself, and all her unspoken sins were forgiven. Jesus said nothing about restitution or atonement. "Your sins are forgiven." Period.

The Adulterous Woman (John 8:1–11). Pharisees brought a woman caught in adultery. (No mention of her consort.) Moses said she should be stoned; what did he say? Jesus bent and began tracing in the dirt and said, "Whoever of you is without sin, cast the first stone." Gradually, the accusers skulked away. Jesus looked up. "Has no one condemned you?" She replied, "No one, sir." Jesus said, "Nor do I condemn you. You may go. But from now on, avoid this sin." Again, no questions like the ones I was taught to ask routinely: "What caused this? Problems in your marriage? Any sins of your past life?" No homilies, and surely no anger—only quiet acceptance and the admonition to avoid doing it again.

The Samaritan Woman (John 4:4–40). At the well of Shechem, a woman was surprised that he, a Jew, asked water of a Samaritan. Jesus said, "If only you recognized God's gift and who asks for a drink, you would ask him instead and he would give you living water." Again, the invitation to a freer, richer life. There was an easy, teasing banter between them, but when Jesus asked her to call her husband, she answered, "I have no husband." And he replied (surely with a grin), "True. You've had five, and the man you're with now isn't your husband." But Jesus didn't pursue her promiscuity. Instead, he spoke of something more important: eternal life.

The Prodigal Father (Luke 15:11–32). The clearest insight into Jesus' (and God's—therefore our) treatment of sinners is this story. The only character in both parts is the father, the one the story teller wanted his audience to identify with. When the boy had frittered away half his father's life savings, he *saw* his mistake and headed home, memorizing a confession. But the father saw him "a long way off . . . and was deeply moved." Which implies the father was out there every day, hoping. And the father ran to the boy, not the other way round, threw his arms around him and kissed him, *before* the kid got out a word! "Quick!" his father cried, "Kill the fatted calf. Let's celebrate because my son who was dead is *alive* again!"

So much for justice. The father didn't say, "I want an account of every shekel before you get back into my house!" Not a penance but a *party*! Because the lost sheep was home. The whole gospel: forgiveness and resurrection.

Like so many, the older brother tried to *merit* his father's love, when he'd had it since nine months before he'd ever seen the boy's face. Self-absorption blocked out the whole point.

Peter (John 21). Finally, the first pope—who had apostatized three times in one night, denied Christ with fierce oaths, not to authorities but to servants—faced no inquiry from Jesus into specifics, no exaction of guilt or shame, no compensatory penance. Jesus merely asked—three times—"Do you love me. Are we still friends?"

Beyond Atonement

Which prompts a further suggestion beyond the penal justice

system I grew up with: a concern not for punishment, but for rehabilitation.

A few times, in fifty-plus years as a teacher and drama director, I think I may have gotten it right, used imagination in a crisis rather than the usual penal code. One time I was grading senior AP English essays, I found two that were word-for-word identical. They were each too smart to copy from each other, but on the Internet I found an essay they'd both spent ten bucks for. At the teachers' small Mass next morning, I asked at the prayers to handle a cheating situation the way Jesus would. One first-year teacher texted me after Mass and said it was important—he implied treasonous to evade—that the boys be turned over to the discipline office so it would be on their permanent records. Instead, I met with them separately and asked for an essay, just three paragraphs: What does integrity mean? How does it feel when you lose it? And how do you get integrity back?

One wrote that it was the first time in his life he understood what Christianity means. The other came to confession for the first time since eighth grade.

But the young teacher had gone to the school's president, who called me in and demanded I give the boys' names to the office. I told him what I'd done and why and how they'd responded. He insisted: "All well and good, but." I stayed stubborn. And it still feels very good.

The gospels are abrasively insistent on "losing your life" and "Unless a grain of wheat die" and "dying to self." That's what forgiveness always asks. It means dying to the false self, the remains of the child in us: grabby, petulant, thin skin, nearly autistic. Well lost.

A.A. says, "Resentment's like taking poison and hoping the other guy dies." I bet you have some grudge. Maybe at those who routinely take you for granted. I confess, there still remain people I find it excruciating even to consider forgiving—their cold-bloodedness, their hypocrisy, their condescension, their unloving. Granting them Christian amnesty would detoxify myself. But . . . it's so hard.

Forgiving Yourself

Each time I find myself flat on my face,
I pick myself up and get back in the race.
—Dean Kay and Kelly Gordon (and Frank)

The worst sin of good people like you and me is perfectionism. Lacerating our slightest faults. Even our kindnesses seem never enough. Everything falls humiliatingly short of our expectations. Of course it does. By definition, nothing human can ever be perfect. "If only I hadn't fumbled . . . if only I hadn't said that." Forget the damn "if onlys" (because God does, I think, damn them). If you tried your best, what do you have to apologize for—even to yourself? If you didn't do your best, assess how responsible you were, do something about it, then get on with your life. Brooding on your faults can be just as self-serving and narcissistic as staring in the mirror at your charms. And just as paralyzing. You're wasting time. Pick yourself up and get back in the race.

When you judge your own guilt, you ought to judge as impartially as you'd judge any other good friend, the kind of friend you don't have to pussyfoot with, the kind you can tell the bald truth to. Assess the injury—without letting yourself off too easily, and without treating yourself like a worthless bum. Then *do* something about it: apologize—to God and to the one you've hurt. God forgives, and if your victim refuses forgiveness, at least have the good grace to forgive yourself.

Once you've inventoried your faults and dumped them in confession, leave them there. To keep harping back to them denies any claim you purport to believe in the Christian God. Humble yourself to accept *being* accepted. From then on, if you truly admit the sacredness of your soul—your authentic self—you'll never again degrade it, especially not in silly ways. And once you *own* that sacredness, all moral theology becomes superfluous. Your integrity will take care of itself.

Forgiving God

Surely, the absolute dumbest assertion about God is that we made him up ourselves to smother our fear of death and annihilation. The greatest fool God ever gave breath could have come up with a more congenial model than the God we actually have. Few of us have been as ambushed and sideswiped and disillusioned as old Job, but is there anyone our age who hasn't had enough experience to be certain as death and taxes that God's ways are not our ways?

I've presided at too many teenage funerals to see God only as a cherishing mother. Like any friend—like Job—I felt God betrayed our friendship. (More honestly, my *expectations* of it—as most other friends have.) Every one of those times, kids asked me through their tears, "Help me understand this." When I was grinding my guts to try to understand it myself.

For seven long years in the seminary, I worked like a dray horse and never—not once—got a grade higher than a C. Where's the love in that? Not to mention just fairness? I didn't just work, I prayed with all the ardor of a Buddhist novice. Because I *really* believed that "Whatever you ask in my name" business. Sorry. I had to discover that "No" is, in fact, an answer.

A huge part of my job is as defense counsel for God. That was apparently what all that blissfully forgotten theology was supposed to prepare me for. It didn't. Because the rock-bottom God problem is that this God we offer doesn't play fair. How do we defend him next to the coffin of a teenage suicide, or the bedside of a young father dying of cancer, or holding the hand of a girl unexpectedly pregnant? That's a great deal of a priest's job, isn't it—defending the indefensible?

Which—now that I ponder it—proves the validity and effectiveness of my mediocre grades and the incomprehensible "answers" the church had set me to master. The answer was, "There are no answers!" Not the kind I wanted. Not the kind Job's comforters offered. Not the slice-and-dice rational theses I so pitifully defended in the annual orals. The answer the seminary taught was endurance.

The only answer is trust. In a friend. In someone you know in a quite different way from the way you know calculus or history or dogma.

I now have enough experience of God that I no longer resort to petitionary prayers. I stopped years ago when my mother didn't even know who I was. One time, in the hospital, I leaned over to kiss her, and she started screaming, screaming, and the nurse told me I'd better leave. I went down to the car, put my head on the steering wheel, and just sobbed. I called God every foul name I could conjure. "Goddamn you! I've given you my whole god-damned life. Why can't you let her go?" And God refused. It was the ultimate insight he gave Job: "Where were you when I laid the foundations of the earth? Should I check my plans with *you*?"

I learned from Our Lady at Cana. She didn't say, "What do you intend to do about this wine situation?" Much less, "After all I've done for you." She said only, "They have no wine"—telling him what he doubtless knew, and let him handle it as he chose. Which God will do anyway. We just have to lower our grandiose expectations about God's subservience to us.

One day, walking along a country road, hangin' out with Jesus, I got an epiphany, from a big-bottomed black Labrador retriever. She came up with a stick and sort of insisted I throw it. So I threw the thing till my arm was limp as linguine, and I stopped. Well, she shouldered me, apparently asking if I'd forgotten my place in her universe. Just then, a car came careening down the road, so I grabbed her choke chain and dragged her out of the way, coughing and snarling. When the car had gone, she gave me this bitchy look and trundled off in a hairy huff. At that moment, I grasped a formidable truth. I realized I understood God's motives in refusing my requests and jerking my chain about as well as that black Lab understood mine. Humbling.

There is the ultimate forgiveness: forgiving God—for *being* God—for having plans and purposes he's unable or unwilling to share with us.

That's the insight a crucifix is meant to incite. "Here I am! I'm as human as you. And I am the way, and the truth, and the life. This is the only way to a truer, richer, profounder life."

This is his final lesson: "Father, into your hands I surrender all that I am."

23.
Eternal Life—Now

*We're depending on God; he's everything we need.
What's more, our hearts brim with joy since
we've taken for our own his holy name. Love us,
God, with all you've got—that's what we're
depending on.*
                              —Psalm 33:20–22 (MSG)

Forty years ago, when I was in *The Exorcist*, I was a guest on the *Today* show. During a commercial break, Barbara Walters leaned toward me and whispered, "You're obviously an intelligent man. *How* can you be a *priest?*" As if I had a PhD sheepskin in one hand and a strangled rooster in the other. I answered, "Because it gives me so much joy!" She sniffed and turned away. "I don't know what that means." At the time, she made over a million smackerolas a year, and she didn't know what joy meant.

When I told that story in class the other day, for the first time ever, a student asked, "What *is* joy?" From the top of my head I could only answer, "It's an exuberance about being alive, a conviction that what you're doing is doing some good—a gut feeling you know who you are and where you're heading." Inadequate, but the best I could do on the spot.

Then another one turned it into a graced ambush: "How to you *find* joy?" I'd been warned: "Always be ready to make your defense to anyone who demands from you an accounting for the hope that is in you" (1 Peter 3:15). "One way is taking a genuine ownership of your own death. Realizing the number of days you'll wake up is a finite number, so every one of them is precious. 'Oh, God! Another *day!*' Or look at life from the other end: I needn't have been born. After all the miscarriages, my parents could have given up. Granted if I'd never been born I'd never know the difference, but I *was* born! Think of all the people I might never have known and loved! How *lucky* I am!" When I'm blessed to realize that, I feel joy.

But that was only a pro temp response. The kids I teach have always been a temptation from God for me to rethink "stuff" I'd always assumed I understood. I've *felt* joy, but do I know what it really means and how to find my way there?

What did Jesus mean by "eternal life"? Aliveness even death can't threaten.

You can see a difference between "joy" and "hope," which is quiet confidence that ultimately everything is going to be alright. Hope says, "There's no way in hell I'm gonna win, by God I'm not gonna quit." Singing on the deck of *The Titanic*, giggling in a cancer ward, hunkering in a foxhole.

I used to confuse joy with "happiness"? But joy's *more* than happiness.

Happiness

Remember the little bright-eyed girl in the subway car and all the people around her with dead-ended eyes. What got lost? More important: Is whatever got lost irretrievable?

Happiness is the one thing everybody wants. The Declaration of Independence affirms our right to pursue it: God-given, inalienable, self-evident. But does anybody have the slightest idea what happiness *means*? A vague goal is unachievable. ("Oh, uh, . . . I'm goin' *somewhere*, that's for sure!") How will we know when we arrive where happiness is? Or that we haven't sauntered right past it? Or even that we haven't been carrying it with us all along?

"Happiness" is as elusive as all those other quicksilver realities we value so much and understand so little: love, faith, spirituality, God. In my waning years I find I haven't gotten any of them boxed in quite as neatly as I'd thought. All I was so sure I knew I apprehend only as a smear, in a glass, darkly.

Most media victims (the sad grown-ups in the subway) have the ineradicable conviction that, if they can just pile up enough money, fame, sex, and power, they'll be happy. But if that's true, how to explain Elvis, Marilyn, and those enviable folks who "had it all" but sedated themselves with drugs (from life) for years and finally killed themselves? Because they were so *happy*?

Others fantasize happiness as being unbothered: no deadlines, no expectations, the stuff of Caribbean travel posters. But "happiness" can't be the blissful, carefree life of a child. At puberty, our bodies removed that option. It can't mean being unperturbed, because all the other porcupines have quills and different agendas. And any story without uninvited witches isn't worth telling—or living. Nor can happiness mean being free of heartbreak, because love opens us to inevitable loss down the line. Nor can it mean merely "getting by," coping year after year, then dying. That's merely not unhappiness. Whatever definition of "happy" we form has to factor in the inevitables: work, others' expectations, mislaid plans, suffering.

When people say, "Y'all have a nice day, now, ya hear?" what do they mean? Don't run into any upsetting people? Don't break a heel? Don't run into anything to challenge your ingenuity, courage, stamina, and force you to grow? And *don't* have children! If that's what being happy means, we're all stranded on the wrong planet. There's no way there from here.

Yet aren't those fuzzy estimates of happiness at the core of our unexamined intuitions about it? Don't we want that for our children? Free of care, worry, sin; surrounded by loving, understanding, forgiving people; secure from betrayal and tragedy and numbing routine? But Eden went out of business years ago. If that's our unspoken goal, we're doomed to unhappiness.

Meanwhile at least those of us stranded in big cities have to steel ourselves to shrieking sirens, road rage, insolent graffiti, surly self-absorption. Rarely do we gasp in distress any more over tabloid stories of murderous parents, sadistic policemen, drug-addled athletes, derelict homeless, unwed children who beget children, dead-ended lives. We've developed a high tolerance for inhumanity, for soullessness. A good deal of pop music seems concussive, primal, enraged, soul-numbing.

And "Why is fulfillment always in the future?" An all-knowing God hardly needs to make life one hellish test after another to see who's worthy of heaven. And meanwhile we're all the proverbial jackass with a stick tied atop his head, a carrot dangling inaccessibly at the far end? That blasphemous god would be a sadist, unworthy of respect, much less worship.

The wise Greeks believed genuine happiness (success and fulfillment) doesn't reside in the feelings at all, nor must it await heaven, nor is it found in accumulating property, highs, or notches on one's gun. Happiness resides rather in the soul. In fact, their word for "happiness" was *eudaimonia*, "having a good soul," and Hebrews and early Christians believed happiness was holiness—being whole—which we can understand from all its synonyms: all-together, unfragmented, consistent, focused, integrated, harmonious, and—perhaps best—fully alive. A good farmer's life, for instance, seems a chaotic jumble of unrelated tasks: plow, drain the oil, milk, pray for rain, pick up the kids. Yet it all has a wholeness: making things grow. That's what I meant in class by knowing who you are, where you're going. You're self-triangulated so you always know "where you are." It's what the present patois means by "having all your (*beep!*) together." We'll never be happy until we imitate the God in whose image we're made: Bringing cosmos out of chaos, bringing all the seemingly unharmonious parts into a oneness: a life.

Happiness, then, independent of feelings, means being serene in the face of the unchangeable, courageous before the changeable, and wise enough to know which is which—being "at home" within oneself and within the web of human relationships in which we find ourselves, however disconcerting. By that definition, people walking to the gas ovens of Buchenwald, heads high, firmly grasping their undaunted souls, were happy. Conversely, Hitler, capering at Napoleon's tomb over the humiliation of France, wasn't happy. Just momentarily feelin' good.

What the sad subway folk left behind is the challenge to grow as human beings—which was precisely the reason the founding fathers insisted on free public schooling. They settle for a "realistic" acceptance of what seems irresistibly "the way things are," adjust to the humdrum, even to the antihuman, which then becomes the norm, the stunting we share with everybody else. After a while we don't even notice how impoverished we've become. But somewhere inside we feel what Peggy Lee captured: "Is that all there is?" There's *got* to be more. That cry comes from the soul within each of us—that spark of the divine each of us encloses.

I don't *have* a soul; I *am* a soul. I *have* a body, which I trust my soul will survive. There are many words that cluster around the idea of the human soul: psyche, spirit, self, who-I-am, conscience, essence, character, life force. "Soul" reflects the entire core of one's personal existence: the whole living being of an individual and that self's *reason* for living, a unique storyline, a lifeline. And most ignore it. Surely schools and churches do.

Awakening that soul, understanding it, and challenging it to grow is what human life is all about! If I haven't even begun that process, I haven't even begun to live. Rocks fulfill their purpose just by sitting there; the key is in the way God made them. Buttercups and bananas fulfill their divine purpose by feeding, growing, reproducing, looking beautiful. Spiders fulfill their purpose by spinning webs and retrievers by chasing sticks. If God sends a message about what will make us happy, written in the way we're made, different from other animals, then the secret of happiness is in the human soul: *learning, loving, growing.*

What separates us, objectively, from other beasts is that, unlike them, we can grow more intensely human. It's obvious Pope John Paul II was more profoundly human than Saddam Hussein. We can crack open our horizons of learning and understanding, expand the limits of our caring. We can push upward on that scheme of human growth from fear and hope of reward to empathy and kindness to those within our reach, then beyond even that into eternal life—not postponed to some future heaven, but here and now! Or not.

Happiness comes from exploiting our human nature. Or we're free to leave that divine potential fallow: become silent drudges, student zombies, soap opera addicts, managerial robots, mercenaries, hit men. Or free, as far too many good, unhappy people do, merely to "get by." Survive instead of thrive. Apathy isn't the most dramatic form of suicide; just the most common. Butterflies who find the cocoon too comfortable and flying too risky.

Proverbs 6 says, "How long will you sit there dribbling your time away, moping and wishing your life were otherwise? You are imprisoned in your dreams of might-have-been, self-condemned to circumvent the truth. Make a life from what you have and are. Or die." And St. Teresa wrote, "Strive, and strive, and strive; we were meant for nothing else." And Albert Camus said, "The struggle itself toward the heights is enough to fill one's heart. One must imagine Sisyphus happy." Wisdom is the serenity that lets you metabolize any trauma.

The soul contented to strive and not arrive finds, after a time, our grimmest crises are our greatest graces, invitations to more abundant life: a girl having her first period, a boy rejected from a team, a man uprooted from a job he'd loved, a woman bereft of husband and children. It's the call of God to Abraham, to Noah, to Moses, to Jesus' first disciples: "That was then; this is now. Leave behind 'the way things always were' and come out on the road with me. We can do it *better*." The wise soul has been galvanized by suffering enough to realize that, in the end, what seems the wrath of God is the love of God, assessed by a fallible fool.

That soul self—the inner character—is what I make of what's been done to me. I see all the truths of my life and say, "That's all right and true. Where do we go from here?" As Dag Hammarskjold put it, "For everything that has been, 'thanks'; for everything to come, 'yes.'"

Once we make peace with those facts, we can get down to the business of living—abundantly—in what time we have, with the parsnips or the spumoni we have on our plates right now. And you don't bother that much about what life after death will be like; you're too busy making sure there's life before death.

I am as fulfilled as I can be, for now.

Joy

Happiness, I think, may be the calm rock from which joy emerges, as life came from lava, and fish from ferns, and anthropoids from apes. The difference, I think, is exuberance—superliveness—enviable, contagious vitality—delight in being alive! Not just a momentary feeling. Not even just a "state" of soul. It's a *passion*—deeper than any feeling, more vibrant than any "state."

Think of the difference between a circle and a sphere, between studying atoms and dancing with them, between theology and a connection to God. Joy is the Holy Spirit who tamed the chaos, quickened the Son in Mary's womb, reenlivened him in the tomb, exploded inside all the disciples on Pentecost.

Joy doesn't stand a chance in what Pope Francis calls "complacent yet covetous hearts in feverish pursuit of frivolous pleasures, blunted consciences." The only purpose in purgatory is to recondition the minds and hearts of puritans, bean counters, fault finders, a kind of makeup course to prepare them to deal with unconditionally loving and being loved. Without it, heaven would fry their soul circuits. "Stop *hugging* me, you *pervert!*" Heaven would be hell.

Like happiness, joy isn't something you can actively "pursue" as an entity in itself. Both are by-products of other pursuits.

The Hebrew scripture uses "joy" for release from enslavement, for wine, sex, marriage, birth—all the places in life where even nonchurchgoers suddenly realize there's a reason for sacraments. Some of us are so zapped with the transcendent lurking in stars and storms and babies' fingernails and being needed that we get a sacramental fix every single day. That's joy.

The gospel exemplifies joy at the return of a lost sheep, lost money, lost children. Angels apparently never lose hold of joy because they're looking at God all the time. Christianity accepts that notion—that happiness comes from having a good soul, in harmony with all the other souls, but it goes much further, to joy. The Kingdom is not static, living at peace with one's neighbors; it needs active engagement in their betterment: healing, as Jesus did, especially the undeserving. For the world, happiness is security: hedges, insurance, police. For the Kingdom, happiness is risk. Not comfortable stasis, but the inner peace of the tightrope walker, the helmsman, those who defuse bombs, terminal ward nurses. Comfort seems the product of encounter groups—a placebo; Christianity is anything but. Gospel parables about hiding one's light and burying one's talents preclude that. As Kazantzakis wrote, Christ is not "Welcome!"; Christ is "Bon voyage!"

To paraphrase Jesus' contrast between the world and Kingdom: I come not to consume, but to be consumed. Or as John Donne put it, "And I, except You enthrall me, never shall be free, nor ever chaste, except You ravish me."

If we want to be useful, it follows unavoidably that, to be joyful, fulfilled, we have to be used. According to Jesus, joy comes from surrendering to God and one's neighbors. "I'm here to bring out the goodness in you, the decency, the healing." What Gandhi called *satyagraha*: the force of the soul that challenges another soul to come spiritually alive. Even in a hospital bed, I'm useful; if I'm willing to swallow my pride and offer my need, my very presence says, "Here's a chance for you to reach out and love." The panhandler serves a purpose: "Here I am, an invitation to open yourself. But is this an openhearted gift, or do you limit how I can spend it?"

Most people settle for a definition of themselves and their lives rather than a meaning. "I'm a fifty-five-year-old black Catholic widow who teaches fifth grade." Definition finds a self as a pastiche of external roles. Meaning is far less clear-cut, yet far larger and more exhilarating. Tennyson: "I am a part of all that I have met." St. Paul: "I live, no longer I, but Christ lives within me." We open up the taproot self who weaves all those disparate surfaces into a vivified and vivifying wholeness.

Happiness and joy aren't "insights" you learn from painstaking research, not a problem to be solved but a realization to be experienced. It's not enough to "know" you're happy. Somehow you have to feel it, know it not in the way you know your checking account is balanced but in the way you know you're loved. It has to be *interiorized* into a conviction. And that means you need time to pray, or at least to ponder.

Purposefully to withdraw from the neon and noise, the bills and imbroglio, is not only salutary but necessary. Out among hills hunching green or in rainbow canyons or before the diapason of crashing waves, nature humbles us into realizing someone else is in charge. Yet, despite the fact that, before the illimitable universe, we are no more than whispers in a hurricane, we are *chosen*—to do what we can.

To find genuine peace—happiness, wholeness, wisdom, joy— there has to be time for it, "Sabbath time" during which we let go of analyses and coping, surrender mastery for mystery, become willing to "be taken in." Before God, no matter our sex, we are all "feminine," pregnable. God comes to us every day, as to Our Lady, and says, "Conceive my Son in you today." Sadly, most of us are too busy trying to prove ourselves, to ourselves, to do what we were made to do.

Life isn't a Sisyphean sequence of tests from God to keep challenging our submission and endurance, a contest whose only reward is knowing you haven't quit. It's a journey, an odyssey. We're going someplace. That's our purpose: to keep becoming more human, cracking the horizons of our knowing and loving. And, in the going, we're already there.

In Philippians (4:4–9), Paul says, "All I want is you, joyful, always happy in the Lord! I repeat: I just want your joy. Make your kindness obvious. The Lord is at your shoulder. Put aside all anxieties . . . and you will know that peace of God which is beyond human capacity to encompass. Fill your minds with everything true, everything noble, everything pure and good, everything lovely and honorable, everything virtuous and worthy of praise. And God's peace will find you."

24.
And Then?

When I stand before God at the end of my life, I would hope that I would not have a single bit of talent left, and could say, "I used everything you gave me."
—Erma Bombeck

What do we do for an encore?

When I was first ordained, I had to give a homily on the Ascension. I wanted to say something *really* new, so I sat down and meditated. My imagination got me so realistically into that scene I felt the dust between my toes and smelled the other apostles' sweat. Jesus took us up a hill, said good-bye, and began to rise. About fifty feet in the air (where artists capture it). Nothing new there. So something impelled me to let him *keep* going. Up, up, like a missile in slow gear.

At that point, the left lobe of my brain (where I store my reasoning equipment and knowledge of science) began asking unsettling questions of my right lobe (where I store my imagining tools and knowledge of religion). Did Jesus go through the Van Allen Belt? Was he radioactive? Did he sail through the endless cold of space till he finally came to the thinnest membrane between the universe and heaven and go through, *boop*! like through a self-sealing tire? And there he was in this great golden city—like the ogre's castle atop the beanstalk? But, beyond time and space, where do they mine all that gold? (Not to mention all the oysters for the pearls on those gates—plus all the coal to keep hell fires burning.) And if Jesus went "up" to heaven from Jerusalem, an Australian would go "up" in exactly the opposite direction. And never the twain shall meet. My earliest training had frozen both brain lobes back in the first century. Back to the drawing board.

We know so much more about the cosmos than the scripture writers. We know now the earth isn't really an island floating on the waters, covered by the great crystal bowl of firmament beyond which lies heaven. We know that, if God preexisted the universe of time and space, God dwells in a dimension of reality where everything temporal and physical has neither meaning nor purpose. God has no genitals and thus is not male. Angels don't need wings to get about. Devils don't sport tails or use pitchforks. But how do we deal with realities like heaven, hell, purgatory—and God himself!—when the only tools we have are our space-time-bound experiences? Maybe Hindus and Buddhists have the right idea. In their view, the ultimate reality does exist, but in such an unimaginably different way from our existence, we can say nothing true about "it" or its environs. Anything we say about such a being is so far from the actuality as to be closer to a lie than to the truth. You can't even legitimately use the word "is" about such a being in any remote sense like the way we use it about anything else we know.

Still, God gave us complex intelligence to try to understand things, even if our approximations are "straw," as Aquinas reputedly said, compared to the reality. That's why God made us symbol spinners, metaphor makers, trying to make realities we can't actually see concretely—like tiny solar systems for atoms, a wedding ring for commitment, a parchment for intellectual achievement (or endurance). None of the symbols *are* the reality (thus Jews and Muslims forbid most of them), nor are they, even in the remotest sense, much like the reality. But they're a helpful placebo for the inquiring mind. And if Jesus used analogies to help explain his message, we're in good company when we try them, too. They help us understand a bit better something we don't really understand in terms of things we do. Symbols are (to use a metaphor) like the ACE bandages the Invisible Man wrapped around himself to be seen. Like trying to "explain" color to a blind person. "Red is the burning sensation of sucking a hot cinnamon jawbreaker." That's not "it," but it's better than nothing at all.

The Hebrew scriptures try that in the book of Daniel (7:9–14), about as close as they get to a "picture" of God, clad in snow-white clothes on a fiery throne, sitting upon the clouds of heaven. And the whole book of Revelation pictures heaven as "the New Jerusalem," the most opulent city the author could conceive. On the very rare occasions hell arises, the analogy is to Gehenna, where Jerusalem burned its trash. Again and again, Jesus used metaphor to describe the Kingdom of heaven as a wedding banquet where (presumably) no one has too much to eat or drink, the conversations are never dull, and everybody dances like Fred and Ginger.

Unfortunately, because we still carry a reptilian brain stem, hell is much more interesting than heaven (to say nothing of its usefulness to preachers to panic us to piety). But we owe our "understanding" of hell far more to the imagination (and prejudices) of Dante and the fervor of Irish Jansenist preachers than to the meager evidence of the scriptures. The atheist Jean-Paul Sartre has, for me, a far better reimaging of hell than Dante: three people who *detest* one another forced to share a hotel room for all eternity, without the possibility of murder or suicide. I can think of at least *twenty* people I'd do just about *anything* required to avoid sharing that fate.

But if God is both merciful and just, there has to be some kind of accommodation for people who simply don't want to go where someone besides themselves is the focus of attention and, as we saw, some reschooling for those who—for one reason or other—lived joyless lives.

Sometime, during a coffee break or cocktail hour, ask the people you're with, "What do you think heaven will be like?" Try to lure them away from the standard dumb images. Surely if it's heaven, it can't be boring, static, not for creatures born as inquisitive as we've been. How do they suspect God will find ways to "keep the joy going"?

The best reimaging of the afterlife I know is C. S. Lewis's series of vignettes called *The Great Divorce*. It begins in a gray town where everything is grim and everyone surly. But at any time you can take a bus that lands in a beautiful meadow, a kind of staging area for heaven, up in the beautiful mountains. Each one is greeted by a Solid One, someone from their past, who tries to coax them to jettison their self-absorption, stop telling lies to themselves about themselves—and believing them, and yield center stage to the only one who deserves it: God. Some do, and for them, their sojourn in the gray town has been purgatory. Others cling to their narcissism, get back on the bus, and return. For them, the gray town is hell. Not the fascinating sadistic punishments of Dante, just plain boredom, mean-spiritedness, frustration. But, as Milton says, "Better to reign in hell than serve in heaven."

Even if the scriptures say nothing much (that I can find) about purgatory, I think plain common sense dictates there must be such a "place." There must be some purgation (not fire but like the slow anguish of self-discovery in a psychiatrist's office) for those who die incapable of joy. People who have spent lives insulated from others, self-protective and self-delusive, hearts as hard and pitted as the seeds of peaches. The cranks, the fainthearted too afraid of being hurt to love, those who buried their thousand talents rather than risk losing them. How disoriented would they be in heaven? Like Laplanders suddenly transported to the Sahara.

Ah, but what of heaven? My mom used to say just squeaking in was enough. After the life she led, if that's all Mom got, if she didn't get first-class accommodations, I'm not too sure I want to go there. An alcoholic old religious who'd failed some god-awful exam back in the seminary and was thus allowed only a second-class kind of final vows said to me once, weeping, "To think after I've tried so hard all my life, I'll have a lower place in heaven than the fully professed." If rule makers have the keys of the Kingdom, I suspect heaven is a rather sparsely populated and sterile state of being.

In Alice Sebold's novel *The Lovely Bones*, the narrator tells her story from heaven where, if she chooses to frolic in the rain, it rains; if she wants to cavort in the fields, the sun radiates warmth. But she seems to have an "inordinate" preoccupation with what's still going on back at home and the capture of her murderer. And she has an unusual touchstone: "There wasn't a lot of b——t in my heaven." In Thornton Wilder's *Our Town*, the dead sit placidly in straight-backed chairs in the cemetery, gradually letting go of the world, as the people they love let go of them. Perhaps that's true, that the recently dead hover around trying to interfere, but I can only hope that's not the way it is. Let them get on with their joy. That's what love does: sets free.

Whatever it is, I find it hard to accept a static heaven, sitting there while the fussbudgets fine-tune the Beatific Vision. God has so conditioned us to growth, to evolution, to look for something better, that I have a notion (a hope) heaven will be a place of learning more and more. I'd really like to be able to do all the things I "never had time for" here, like understanding classical music. To learn patience and shed myself of workaholism in order to just sit and fish. (Perhaps that would be purgatory.) I'd really like to talk to God (or some trustworthy assistant) about a lot of mysteries I've spent a lifetime trying, vainly, to unlock, like why God created a world in which innocents can suffer, why the Holy Spirit allowed the church to be so manifestly imperfect, why my mother took eight years to die. And both my teacher and I will have no impatient rush to closure in unraveling the truth.

Ignorantly, I used to think Eastern understanding of the eternal was soul-suicidal, that the purpose of life, to them, was to eliminate the self so totally it would be ready to be absorbed into the oversoul. Then I read a sentence that shocked me. In achieving Nirvana, it said, the droplet is not absorbed by the All; the droplet absorbs the all! That's getting closer to less unsatisfying.

As we've seen, I believe the nearest approximation we can get to the ultimate, to heaven, has something to do with light. What if there *were* a reality faster than light? It would be so hyperenergized, it would be at rest. Like God. So incredibly fast, it would be everywhere at once. Like God. And if you break open the tiniest kernel of matter, what do scientists say you will find? Nonextended energy. Like God. When I had my most intense encounter with God, I could describe it only as "like drowning in light." So many who return from near-death experiences describe it as seeing some trusted figure incandescent with light.

Perhaps the dead are something *like* neutrinos, particles, with no discernible mass or electrical charge, that whiz all around us, at every moment. They pass gleefully through the whole earth without being slowed down. (This is hard science now.) If neutrinos were intelligent and caring and full of joy, perhaps they may be like the dead, zipping around for the sheer zest of it, like children. And if they now live in a dimension unchecked by time and space, where God dwells, they can be anywhere they choose—closer to us now even than they were in this life! But not, I hope, forced to slow down for our sake.

All this is, of course, supposition—imagination working on belief that heaven, hell, and purgatory exist. If Dante and Lewis and Sartre can, why can't you and I?

Whatever heaven turns out to be, it isn't going to be some majestic panoply planned by liturgists or sitting on clouds twanging harps. Whatever gives the best part of you joy, that's what it'll be. If you love babies, you can take care of all the new ones who arrive. If you love to sing and dance, do it and never drop. But what about me? My great joy is to tempt people to *live*. Maybe be a purgatory teacher. I'm equipped.

So many parents are needlessly troubled about their children—or spouses or siblings—who find Mass no longer worth the effort. "At death, will we never see them again?" Just like albed people drifting aimlessly around on clouds so dear to cartoonists, I find the image of St. Peter at the pearly gates, the Code of Canon Law on a lectern at his left elbow, that legendary big account book at his right, checking passports, pretty dumb. And judging from the cavalier way Jesus handled such wanderers as the whore who wept on his feet, the adulterous woman, the prodigal son, the cowardly first pope, I can't imagine an omniscient God needing an MRI of the soul. Nor could I bring myself to worship a God less merciful than I am.

According to Jesus, we're going to be seated at the Great Banquet with lots of folks *we* surely wouldn't have invited had we been the host's social secretary. There'll be people welcomed "up" there who were barred from the Eucharistic table "down" here. Apostate Simon Peter at the head of the table next to the host, runty Zaccheus, garish hookers, Dutch Schultz, and a few gangbangers. People who were divorced, married gays, suicides, lots of heretics, and sincere atheists. Knowing God's penchant for upsetting expectations, I imagine I'll be seated between a starchy former puritan and a drooling graffiti artist.

Flannery O'Conner described Mrs. Turpin's vision of heaven as she squatted by a pigsty.

She saw the streak as a vast swinging bridge extending upward from the earth through a field of living fire. Upon it a vast horde of souls were tumbling toward heaven. There were whole companies of white trash, clean for the first time in their lives, and bands of black n——s in white robes, and battalions of freaks and lunatics shouting and clapping and leaping like frogs. And bringing up the end of the procession was a tribe of people whom she recognized at once as those who, like herself and Claud, had always had a little of everything and the God-given wit to use it right. She leaned forward to observe them closer. They were marching behind the others with great dignity, accountable as they had always been for good order and common sense and respectable behavior. They alone were [singing] on key. Yet she could see by their shocked and altered faces even their virtues were being burned away.

God isn't "up there" or "far off." God is right here, closer to us than our own pulses. Find a quiet place and empty yourself of all the pressures and demands of your workaday life ("the real world"). We're like wombs—expectant potential, like the void before creation: fertilities awaiting their quickening. Not passive, receptive. Open that God-sized emptiness in yourself and let The Really Real world flood in. Don't ask anything or try to solve any problems. Just rest there, at peace, "at home."

25.
Resilience

*Dostoevski said once, "There is only one thing
I dread: not to be worthy of my sufferings."
These words frequently came to my mind after
I became acquainted with those martyrs whose
behavior in [Auschwitz], whose suffering and
death, bore witness to the fact that the last inner
freedom cannot be lost. They were worthy of their
sufferings; the way they bore their suffering was
a genuine inner achievement. It is this spiritual
freedom—which cannot be taken away—that
makes life meaningful and purposeful.*
—Viktor Frankl

At our age, we're quite content to settle for whatever lessons
unmerited suffering has *already* offered to open us to. Long ago,
we (reluctantly) accepted the "fittingness" of some sufferings—
like hangovers and speeding tickets. But now that we've accumulated all those allegedly profitable experiences, we do have more
time and leisure to distill out the "essence" within them all, to
satisfy ourselves that they weren't just "stuff we went through."
To find and grasp the wisdom toward which our lives have led us.
Were our sufferings "valuable"?

What *legitimates* suffering? What purpose and meaning could a
provident God have for inflicting it on us? How do we find value
in negations?

Physical evils (hurricanes, impaired children, death itself) and
moral evils (war, rape, dishonesty) either have an intention—a purposeful deity whose reasons our minds are too time-space bound
to fathom, or they are purposeless—the result of evolution's stum-
bling one blind step too far and coming up with a species that
knows its every trial and triumph is ultimately futile.

In a godless reality, the definitive answers we yearn for don't exist. But even in a reality whose God has purposes we can't clearly read, all we can discover are "clues," as Peter Kreeft states in *Making Sense out of Suffering*. "Questioning," Kreeft writes, "is equally far removed from both dogmatism (thinking you have all the answers) and skepticism (believing there are no answers). Neither the dogmatist nor the skeptic questions. Dogmatism is intellectual pride and skepticism is intellectual despair."

Suffering and Value

"Suffering" here covers the spectrum, not only catastrophes from flood to cancer, or the sudden jolts of accidents, betrayal, heartbreak, but also the less dramatic yet real distress provoked by what Erik Erikson calls natural crises or disequilibriums by which our bodies invite us to live larger lives than we'd planned: birth, weaning, schooling, adolescence, marriage, parenthood, aging— and seeing others through those same painful stages.

Legitimate Suffering

Before the task of validating the *unmerited* suffering that comes from physical and moral evils, consider that third source of suffering, not rooted in evil, physical or moral, but within the self: the inability or refusal to deal with what Jung called *legitimate* (opposed to inculpable). It is aggravation arising simply from being an as-yet-incomplete human being in a world where the law is evolution and the lure is entropy.

In this sense, getting out of bed is suffering, leaving the warm womb of the blankets to face the unexpected. Work is suffering a loss of freedom for a felt purpose: a paycheck, the well-being of one's family, a sense of significance. Living together—from a married couple to a family to a community—is suffering: foreswearing independence, curbing resentments, compromising, because we can accomplish more together than alone. Windsprints and weightlifting are painful, but suffered for a purpose—athletic, cosmetic, hygienic. Learning is suffering, disciplining oneself to persevere with few immediate rewards—which is why so little of it occurs, since those on whom it is inflicted find no felt *purpose* in enduring it.

Any significant change is, in its broadest sense, suffering: a loss. Growth itself is suffering, since we have to give up a self we were comfortable with in order to evolve a *better* self. But since we live in an ethos that recoils even from inconvenience—much less the troublesome effort to change one's stultifying habits—it's not surprising we live in a society composed in great part of terminal adolescents.

One can pretend to "solve" the question of legitimate suffering either by evading it or by suppressing knowledge of it.

As Carl Jung insists, *evading* the legitimate suffering that comes simply from dealing with the world we were dealt always ends in neurosis—anxiety, obsessions, narcissism, blaming our faults on our personalities rather than blaming our personalities for our faults. "I'm a procrastinator" seems self-justifying, as if it were an incurable disease of which I am a victim.

But living an illusion, lying to oneself and believing the lies, is very hard work. Thus, whatever we accept as a substitute for the truth becomes more painful than the truth. What's more, denying the suffering that comes from facing life as it is, flat on, avoids growth as a human being, since growth is by definition leaving the security of the cocoon in order to fly.

Suppressing suffering involved in facing the truth—drowning it in booze, drugs, witless busyness, "coping with" what is actually changeable—is equally self-destructive. Perhaps the most widespread neurosis is minding one's own business, sticking the thumb in the mouth and letting the rest of the world go by, stingy with one's attention, affection, time, and money.

According to Freud's Pleasure Principle, each individual, each culture, makes a fundamental choice between two options, *eros*, the life wish, or *thanatos*, the death wish. Now our culture seems at first glance head over heels in pursuit of eros and pleasure, yet it is not in the sense Freudians intend "*eros*": welcoming challenge in order to grow. Quite clearly, our society is not in pursuit of heroism but of anesthesia: the passive paradise of the womb, the painless, brainless utopia of *Brave New World*. Even sex is often not a quest for love but for lethe.

Again, as Burger, the psychiatrist in *Ordinary People*, tells the anguished Conrad, "If you can't feel pain . . . you won't feel anything else, either."

Unmerited Suffering

Wisdom is making peace with the unchangeable. We have the freedom to face the unavoidable with dignity, to understand the transformational value *attitude* works on suffering. Frankl writes that in concentration camps, "What alone remains is 'the last of human freedoms'—the ability to choose one's *attitude* in a given set of circumstances.

Are we responsible for our unmerited sufferings? The answer is no. And yes. We are not responsible for our predicament as its cause—cancer or job loss or the death of a child or spouse. Or more trivially, wrinkles, gray hairs, a paunch. But we are responsible for what we do with the effects, with the rubble fate has made of our lives.

The only hand we have to play is the hand God or fate deals us. We need not be victims of our *biological* fate. Stephen Hawking is a good example of a Phoenix risen from ashes. One night the evening news reported a young man receiving his Eagle Scout award. Nothing newsworthy in that, except he was twenty-two and couldn't give an acceptance speech. Instead, his father spoke it as his son pointed to letters on a board atop his wheelchair. He had cerebral palsy: for his merit badge in hiking, he had pushed his chair nine miles, then crawled the rest of the way.

We need not be victims of our *psychological* fate. We are, surely, driven by the winds, but a skillful sailor can use the wind, whereas "I'm doomed" and "I'm nobody" become self-fulfilling prophecies. As Frankl starkly and firmly asserts, "A faulty upbringing exonerates nobody." Those with callous upbringings in shoddy circumstances are in truth victims of others' mistakes, but it is the inescapable burden they were delivered, and they are no more hamstrung by it than the boy with cerebral palsy. Each of our stories is unique, with its own demons and dragons. Accept that and get on with what you have left: you.

We need not be victims of our *situational* fate, immured in its "laws," living a provisional existence, settling for mere "survival." Some who went down on the *Titanic* went down singing. People have gotten off third-generation welfare. Women and men survived Dachau, Auschwitz, the Gulag, Bosnia, Rwanda. And they came through battered but unbowed, with their own souls clasped firmly in their own hands. If such heroism is possible for so many ordinary people, surely it is possible to say "no" to soulless societies and soulless selves, to Gradgrind, to the naysayers and nobodies we're surrounded by. Surely it's possible to say "no" to the shallow values purveyed incessantly by the media.

There is a meaning to "value" here totally unfamiliar in a utilitarian society where "dignity, integrity, altruism" simply won't compute. How much do they pay? But in a life view where one's soul is more indicative of worth than one's bank balance, the fighting alone counts. There is no lost cause if the cause is just. In the going, I'm already there.

Dr. Martin Luther King Jr. wrote,

The value of unmerited suffering [calls us] either to react with bitterness or seek to transform the suffering into a creative force. If only to save myself from bitterness, I have attempted to see my personal ordeals as an opportunity to transfigure myself and heal the people involved in the tragic situation which now obtains. I have lived these last few years with the conviction that unearned suffering is redemptive.

Death and Value

Until we wrap our minds around the *reality* of death—not in the abstract, but as the only infallibly predictable event in each of our futures, we live the illusion we have plenty of time. We can ask ourselves will my savings last, will my children keep safe, will I be happy when I leave my life-defining job? To all those questions you can only do your best and, after that, *que sera, sera*. Nothing is really predictable. Except one thing. We'll all die.

One's death isn't an unpleasant possibility. It's an unpleasant fact. Some find it too morbid to acknowledge. But it doesn't go away. The number of mornings you'll wake up is finite.

Today, death's both obscene and trivialized. On the one hand, we hide it; it happens somewhere else, to someone else. On the other hand, before they graduate from grade school, most children have seen more deaths, real and fictionalized, than a veteran in the army of Julius Caesar. But ignoring or disparaging death is living in an unreal world, and death is inexorably going to intrude on our lives in the deaths of many we love, before death shatters our own illusions about it.

There are three inescapable facts about death: (1) it's inevitable; (2) with the exception of suicides, it's unpredictable; and (3) it's the ultimate test by which we gauge the value of our lives, because it renders everything that has gone before unchangeable. Whether we go on after it or not, death writes an indelible "*finis*" to everything *here*.

Afterlife or Nothing: Transcendent or Immanent

And after death, what? Over eight million ordinary people in America alone have had out-of-body experiences. They describe hovering over the doctors surrounding them in bed, hearing themselves declared dead, then turning to see a familiar figure like a loved one or saint or guru blazing with light, reaching out a kindly hand. Then they come to a boundary and know if they pass they can never return. Often they awake and find a value to life they'd never felt before. But those experiences could be self-induced, wish fulfillment, hallucination.

People have believed heroes like Hercules, Psyche, Orpheus, and Jesus came back from death and appeared to still-living people. But at least in our technological, this world mind-set, such testimonies lump them with people who claim to have been abducted by alien spaceships.

But there is one certitude about the afterlife that brooks no argument: Either we *do* go on, or we *don't*. That's a true and iron dichotomy. Either our souls are capable of transcending the physical limits of our bodies (in *some* way), or we're limited to an immanent life here on earth for as long as we can manage. Either the souls in us are immortal, here and now, independent of their time-bound flesh, or we're just so much refuse waiting to be picked up, and we have no idea of the collection date. A true dualism: either/or; no other alternatives.

There are many—more than a few of them brilliant—who opt for the latter, angst-ridden alternative as the only honest one: we're solely immanent. Continued reality beyond the reach of space/time must be either nonexistent or impenetrable by the rational mind. Therefore, it is as fatuous to ponder the possibility of an afterlife as to ponder whether unicorns gambol on Alpha Centauri. A reasonable argument, not to be gainsaid by simplistic fundamentalist assertions.

But if death is the final moment of our existence, don't say at a wake, "She's in a better life now." She no longer *is;* she's stopped being real. If all each of us is and all we've struggled to achieve as human beings is simply snuffed out—Pfft!—when we have a flat EKG, then Edith Stein and Adolf Hitler got exactly the same reward for a life: annihilation.

That may be more horrifying than the realization of death itself. But if the immanentist option is correct, its conclusion is inescapable. And it has a radical effect on what we think our lives are worth and on all our so-called moral choices. Nietzsche had the answers all along.

If we are this-world limited, then the only templates by which we judge our temporary value are time, space, and what we see as our human accomplishments.

Time

Carl Sagan compresses the history of the universe into a single calendar year, with the Big Bang occurring January 1 at 00:00:01. On that scale, earth did not form till September 14; the first dinosaurs, December 24; first humans, December 31—

at 11 p.m. The last 400 years, from Elizabeth I to Elizabeth II, was one-sixtieth of a second. Your sixty-plus years (if you have that many) begin at 11:59:59:50. Then, Cinderella, the ball's over at midnight. For you.

Space

Some of us are six feet, five inches, some are five feet. Inside a small room, a recognizable difference. Standing next to the Sears Tower, there's not. Big Daddy's ranch looks very big when you ride the perimeter, not when you try to pick it out from a photograph of earth from space. Imagine you could get even farther out, to the edge of the Milky Way galaxy (920 quintillion miles away). You spot this tiny system with, surprisingly, only one sun with a few tiny planets orbiting it. From that vantage point, find the Americas, your city, you. On that objectively undeniable scale, what difference is there between what Hitler was able to accumulate and what you can accumulate? "A wart on a frog on a bump on a log in a hole on the bottom of the sea."

Perspective vaporizes our pretensions to importance.

Human Accomplishments

In each of our sixty-plus years, we will love a lot of people, accomplish "things," leave a legacy. But take a best-case scenario: You've won two Nobel Prizes, one for medicine for curing the common cold, one for literature. You've published forty books, each of them well received, and you've had ten exemplary children: a research chemist, a historian, a ballerina, an Academy Award director, and so forth. Better than any life could hope to produce.

But put your accomplishments against the accumulated accomplishments of human history: the discovery of fire, the invention of the wheel, Alexander's conquests, the *Dialogues* of Plato, Michelangelo's Sistine Chapel ceiling alone, Shakespeare's plays. Put your forty books into the Library of Congress. Place your ten talented children against the 100,000 human beings snuffed out in one earthquake—each of them somebody's child: chemists, historians, ballerinas. Perhaps you will live on in your children, but, in the immanentist reality, you'll be unaware of it.

Your contributions may give you a good feeling, temporarily. But it's an opinion held by trash awaiting collection.

Archibald MacLeish captured the immanentist truth as well as I've ever seen it done, in a sonnet called "The End of the World." He describes a bizarre circus filled with freaks. And then,

> Quite unexpectedly the top blew off:
> And there, there overhead, there, there hung over
> Those thousands of white faces, those dazed eyes,
> There in the starless dark, the poise, the hover,
> There with vast wings across the cancelled skies,
> There in the sudden blackness the black pall
> Of nothing, nothing, nothing—nothing at all.

Blaise Pascal (d. 1662), a mathematician and philosopher, faced that ultimate dilemma. Confronted, he said, with two utterly irreducible options—one of which had to be true, one of which had to be false, one of which was appealing (we go on), one of which was appalling (we are erased)—and having no certain way of knowing which was true, the only sane option was to go with the appealing choice and base one's life on that conviction.

I go toward the doorway of death, skipping. "I'm going to a wonderful, endless party!" If I'm wrong, Friedrich Nietzsche is not going to be on the other side, thumbing his nose: "I *told* you so, *dumkopf!*" If I'm wrong, I'll never find out!

One can argue for the transcendent also from an inner hunger we humans have that, as far as we can see, no other animal shares: We want to *survive*—not just battering at the waves to stay alive as it would, but yearning to survive long before we even face death. Perhaps, as the immanentists claim, that hope is self-delusive. But why are we the only species *cursed*—by our very human nature— with a hunger for which there is no food? No sow snoozing in her ring of piglets has her dreams disturbed by the understanding they'll all one day die. We do. If in fact we will not go on, better to have been born a pig.

Life with its sufferings and death makes *sense* only if this is not the only reality but the *foreground* of another dimension where love is not annihilated by death. Again, only two starkly irreconcilable options: life is an instantaneous flash in a sea of endless darkness, or a dark smudge on an infinite light.

Death and Perspective

Negative as death is, making peace with it has very positive effects in our lives and souls. Before the reality of death, every other value lines up in proper priority, which is why the Roman senate decreed each time a victorious general was accorded a triumph through the streets at the head of his captured booty and slaves, a boy stood behind his back, holding a golden wreath over the great man's head, whispering in his ear, "*Memento, mori!* Remember, you will die!"

Death shows us the value of our days. Diamonds are precious; dirt isn't. Diamonds are scarce, and we have a seemingly endless supply of dirt. Time is precious because it's finite. What matters is not the number of our days but the way we use them.

Death shows us what's important. In the face of death, assaults on our bruisable egos shrivel to true triviality. Wise folk who make peace with death try never to go to bed with a grudge, even when the other was wrong, because there'll come a time when it's too late to say, "I'm sorry." For them, the friendship, however tenuous, is more important than the sick-warm feeling of the grudge.

One time, just as my parents were leaving from a visit when I was studying philosophy, my dad came up to me behind the car, tears in his eyes, and said, "Pray for us, Bill. This last year's been hell." It was the first time, ever, he had shared his weakness with me. He had always been reassuring and unbreakable. Now, I had bought the "unwritten rule" for a long time, but at that moment I didn't give a damn if everybody in that seminary was glued to the windows watching us. I kissed my father. I'm so glad I broke the rule. It was the last time I saw my father alive. How lucky I was to be set free.

With an endless supply of days, without death, *nothing* has any felt value. But accepting death, we see that the values we have been *told* are values—long life, accumulation of goods, human accomplishments—are indeed values, but not the most real values. As Frankl says, "The heroic death of one who died young certainly has more content and meaning than the existence of some long-lived dullard." If death is a doorway and not a dead end, the only thing you can take through it is your soul. And if it is a dead end, time is even more precious to the immanentist than to the transcendentalist. Contrarily, if one genuinely claims belief in Christ, one automatically professes belief in resurrection. And if that is true, one can understand grief at the loss of a loved one. But not for long. Resentment at any loss or betrayal is understandable, but not too long.

In either case, death is the ultimate criterion. As Carlos Castaneda writes, when you are in a seemingly unsolvable quandary, the only sane thing is to "turn to your left and ask advice from your death."

26.
Letting Go without Quitting

I know no more now than I ever did about the far side of death as the last letting-go of all, but now I know that I do not need to know, and that I do not need to be afraid of not knowing. God knows. That is all that matters.
—Frederick Buechner

Evolution is such a consistent pattern in all we know that it seems to be inescapably constitutive of the will of God for us. The God who reveals himself in so many myriad ways seems restless with immobility—in no particular hurry, and yet itching to move onward.

The creation itself suggests a divine discontent with "the way things are." The emergence of the nearly limitless carouse of the universe reveals it, every object following the exact same laws—and yet each one uniquely itself. It shows a Creator who's "into" not only order (like the church we grew up in) but also surprise (like the church we have now).

Then, at least on this planet, came the move from inert matter to vegetative matter, capable of reproducing itself, then a quantum leap to animal matter that can move about, feel pain, sense danger, then (until Christ) the final flowering of the divine restlessness: intelligent matter, capable of self-awareness and abstract understanding, to whom the generous Creator surrendered part of his/her/their own omnipotence with the gift of a free will that can thwart even God's intentions. The existence just of human curiosity and restlessness (until schooling smothers and media corrupts) proves conclusively the divine will doesn't suffer complacent security too long. "It's the old-old-oldest of stories."

The Hebrew and Christian scriptures bear out the same discontent: Noah, Abram and Sarai, Joseph, Moses, David, Jeremiah,

Isaiah, Our Lady, the disciples, Paul—had all been more or less content with their lives, whatever their shortcomings, more or less sure of their surroundings and their direction, when suddenly The Great Surpriser shows up and whistles them out onto the road, uproots all their securities, and dares them to start again. To risk happiness for joy.

The history of the church mirrors the same lesson: the radical breach that invited gentiles into the new people, persecutions, barbarian invasions, schisms, rediscovering Greek wisdom, the Renaissance, disintegration of a unified Christendom, the Enlightenment, contraction of the world into a global village, the secularization of nearly every corner of human life. All seem to reveal a God who loves stories, with their unexpected and unwelcome intrusions, conflict and challenge. He/she/they seem to be sitting back, rubbing their hands, and saying, "Now, what can we make of *this*?"

Joseph Campbell's studies show that exact pattern in myths of all cultures. First, the hero/heroine (Adam and Eve, Theseus, Odysseus, Moses, Psyche, Snow White, Beauty with her Beast, Marco Polo, Columbus, Pilgrim, Tom Jones, Candide, Jane Eyre, Huck Finn, the Joads, Dorothy, Holden Caulfield, *Black Boy*, Luke Skywalker, Harry Potter, *The Kite Runner*) feels a "call." It's a vocation, from some beyond-worldly source that the "victim" is at first reluctant to accept, feeling unworthy. Or simply too damn rooted in unbothered security. But some craggy old sort, male or female, keeps popping up, nudging, each time the hero/heroine has to commit/recommit—freely crossing the next threshold, into another dimension fraught with ordeals and temptations. Here, too, unexpected helpers show up just when the hero/heroine feels finished. Finally, the hero/heroine descends to the ultimate abyss—Hades, Mordor—wherein they're ambushed by insight and are utterly transformed by it. It's only in hell where we discover our true selves, where our souls are ignited into spirits by the everlasting. Then each returns "home," but it's a new, reinvigorated "home," a self, known and possessed. Now able to be shared.

These tales were onto something. What else explains their indestructiability?

Each individual human life mirrors that same tendency: the seismic displacement of birth, the literally mind-blowing discoveries of infancy, the disequilibrium of weaning into childhood independence, the challenge of schooling, the bewildering disorientations of adolescence and the search for a personal identity, the surrender of that autonomy in intimacy and partnership.

The first step in a good marriage is *really* letting go—not just physical but psychological separation from the birth family—leaving behind twenty years of unquestioned customs, a room of your own, parents who always had a handle on things, decades of a shared story. Only fools take the folks on *Everybody Loves Raymond* for sane.

Once the honeymoon's over, and you've started to be comfortable with your double identity, the kids come, and you have to let go of that shared privacy (but without losing it!). Then, after twenty-plus years of them being the focus of that newly wrought matrix of meaning, you have to let them go! They find someone they love more—or at least in a much different way—and that forces everybody to shift gears and start over.

And now we come to the final roundup. Letting go the washboard belly, the lustrous hair, the springy step. The final challenge of life is to establish that you've got the hang of it from all the other lettings-go you rose up to. Can you do it with grace, and serenity, and dignity? Let go of youth, without letting go of life? Then let go even of that—knowing it's only one more transition?

The inexorable pattern *justifies* the hope! Not just the Bible, or just religion, but everything! Death and rebirth have been going on incessantly for at least fourteen *billion* years since the Big Bang. Even now, you can't look anywhere in the universe without seeing it, exploding and reconfiguring.

Starting over is such a consistent character trait of the Creator that anything counter to that inveterate habit would be questionable—like water reversing course uphill. The evolution of inert matter into Shakespeare needed uncountable lettings-go, but it seems undeniable "things" always came out in new improved versions. (Footnote: Way back then, they buried their dead with provisions. That suspicion of a further journey is inveterate, too.)

The same motif threads the history of Judaism and Christianity: slow down/fall apart/reassemble the pieces/start again. How dumb would you have to be to ignore that renewal obsession in our Creator?

Wouldn't such a God have an utter, omnipotent contempt for death negating?

When Jesus triumphed over death and reappeared to his friends, nobody recognized him. And yet, after some moments, they did. He was the same Jesus. And yet he wasn't. Jesus told Mary, "Don't cling to me." I'm not the same. You want me back as I was. But I am so different now that it will take you generations, centuries, millennia before you have even the vaguest grasp of what that means.

Most Sundays of our lives, we've dutifully said, "I look for the resurrection of the dead, and the life of the world to come. AMEN." (The "Amen" says, "I really mean that!")

The only question is whether we really do.

No resurrection without suffering and death, no growth without letting go and saying "yes" to whatever will be. Like scriptural heroes, we must leave feeling "at home" in order to find a new, better "at home." No teacher of adolescents (as I have been for fifty years) will deny that young people cleave like barnacles to the unbothered serenity of childhood and hope to enjoy the privileges of newfound bodies without also embracing responsibility for them. Our whole culture clings to (and hucksters) the hope that we can somehow surmount the inevitable challenge of aging.

The same, I think, is destructively true of the church. So-called 50s Catholics, people who are educated *and* Catholic but not educated Catholics, mourn a Catholicism of certitudes—which contradicts the tolerance for ambiguity that the Creator so obviously desires in us. As with childhood, it was so much easier to accept passive conformity in exchange for the burden of thinking for oneself. But the church they mourn and try to "cling to" is dead, the same but no longer the same. The lack of vocations is an unsettling call to the laity, as it was to all those scriptural heroes. "Come out onto the road with Me. We're going for a newer life!" The meaning of faith has changed. For educated people, blind obedience is no longer sufficient. It needs the support of personal understanding of what "being Catholic" really *means*. And learning in midlife is more difficult than at twenty, because it means first *un*learning, letting go, then reaching to grasp something disquietingly new.

Many vowed religious unconsciously mourn the large, exuberant, dedicated comradeship that originally seduced us into leaving behind all to follow Christ, a vibrant sense of solidarity that sustained us through the training and the early years of our service. But those memories we cling to are dead. Our numbers are waning and aging, no longer capable of that contagious zest that lured and supported us for so many years. And the ideal they embodied has reembodied itself in a new, more challenging call that also requires a different kind of faith from what we'd become used to. It is more like the faith Francis Xavier and Isaac Jogues had to achieve rather than the faith of monks and nuns in their choirs and scriptoria.

Way too many prayers in the Mass were written by people frozen in the 1950s. They implore God to keep our minds fixed away from the degrading values of the world and focused unflinching on the values of "the world to come." But unless I misread Jesus, he insisted that we go out and convert *this* world, wrench its startling powers back into the direction they were destined for.

> *Jesus's resurrection is the beginning of God's new project—not to snatch people away from earth to heaven but to colonize earth with the life of heaven. That, after all, is what the Lord's Prayer is about.*
> —Bishop N. T. Wright

Okay, so the world is a rat's nest of screwed-up "values," self-anesthesia, superficiality, exploitation. Utter chaos. Which is precisely what God started with!

"Now, what can we make of this?"

An old story tells of a lone climber just about to reach the crest when he slips, sliding through the gravel till he grabs hold of a tough branch hanging over the abyss. "Help!" he shouts. "Is